THE PRAYER OF MOSES

*Finding Fellowship
with God*

SANDRA QUERIN

Paperback ISBN 978-1-960007-38-4
eBook ISBN 978-1-960007-39-1

Published by
Orison Publishers, Inc.
PO Box 188
Grantham, PA 17027
www.OrisonPublishers.com

Unless otherwise identified, scripture quotations are from the King James Version of the Bible.

Dedication

I dedicate this work to my blessed babies,
Donny and Cynthia, who for the sake of watching the
Lord pull Moses and me through the Red Sea,
suffered many burnt meals and missed events.

Table of Contents

Foreword

It has been a while, quite a while, since I have had the pleasure of reading a book that was so engaging, convicting and healing. What Sandra has done here is nothing short of amazing. She takes us down a road of three-part harmony into the mysterious and powerful life of Moses, which I am fairly certain you have never walked before. She clearly has a grasp on what it means to trust Jesus and pass relationships up for fellowship with Him. This book is a favorite, and I quote it often. You will not be disappointed as you fall deeply in love with her writing style and the phenomenal truths revealed in these pages.

Ron Luce, CEO and cofounder of Teen Mania Ministries, Inc.
Garden Valley, Texas, 2004

Introduction

Moses…the word seems to linger in the air. His life reaches out to us from across the ages declaring a friendship that was forged in the midst of challenging and uncertain circumstances.

From the crushing insecurity that fought his faith to the trial of his own heart before an unworthy jury of kinsmen, Moses is an example of a man who kept pursuing God. In his own pursuit to forsake a relationship with this God whom he feared, to embrace fellowship with this God whom he longed to truly serve, Moses just keeps showing up.

While standing before the burning bush, still exhaling the fumes of his rejection and pain, this reluctant vessel wrestled with God in the debate of the ages. Somewhere in the midst of his scarred life, he finally found the value of standing still and knowing God.

The burning bush, and all it represented, was more than a miracle; it was a declaration of God to Moses, a covenant of how He was going to operate. His weapon of choice? Power! This power was exclusive to God, and He would refuse to let it be manipulated by any man. Moses would find out, as we all must, that we cannot control God. From the plagues, through the Red Sea and right over to his death by design, Moses walked in a favor that went past his inabilities and pain.

In this book we shall discover the elements of the life of Moses in three distinct parts: the Man, the Vessel and the Friend.

1 From his birth to the burning bush, we see him as a man, fragile and unsure, becoming a "carrier" of the

spirit of rejection, which creates strongholds of insecurity and fear in his life. We see him attempt to obey
God, miss God and then run to find Him.

2 As the Lord takes him from the plagues to the promises, we see him as a vessel of God, learning faith and
knowing trust. When he learns the difference between
faith and trust, he is able to rise up as a vessel of honor
and forsake a "called" lifestyle for a "chosen" one.

3 As Moses wanders down the road from the exodus
to exile, we begin to know him as the friend of God,
carrying His heart to a rebellious people, leaning on
God and having compassion for a people who attempt
to destroy him.

As a man, we will find that Moses had many ailments; he lent himself to depression and apathy. He was someone riddled with rejection, which produced vast amounts of fear and insecurity that fought
to handicap him. We find ourselves, even if just for a moment, relating to him as he attempts to walk past who he is to gain who God is.
It is a difficult path, and he fails more times in the beginning than
he succeeds. No matter what God does for him, it's just not enough;
his insecurities and pain are too great, then it happens. He is faced
with Pharaoh and the power of his magicians. Will he remain a man
or become a vessel? It is the question many of us ask for years, never
moving forward. God provoked Moses to go forward, for He wanted
the end result of a vessel: He wanted a friend.

The Prayer of Moses will find and uproot the stronghold of rejection in your life and teach you the difference between faith and
trust! Come and walk beside Moses to see firsthand the evolution of
his heart and how it took him from being a reluctant vessel to a ten-
der friend who walked in the absolute favor of a mighty God. His
life shouts one glaring truth: even when we are dragging around
our rejection and pain, when our lack meets God's favor, we can do
mighty things!

In the end, Moses would become part of the "uncommon club"
that would see him in the Transfiguration of Christ because of this

one abundant reality: he was able to walk away from who he was and walk into who God is. All of this from a man who was rejected, depressed, fearful, insecure, apathetic and forsaken—yet willing to believe that God could raise him up, and He did…right up over to the other side of the Red Sea!

May Jesus Christ, who always emerges victorious in the midst of our pain, show Himself strong in you today. I pray you feel His healing touch as you go forward through these pages.

The Prayer of Moses

Lord, help me to destroy the root of rejection in my life, so that Your favor will abound upon me! I forgive those who planted the seeds of rejection in me, and Lord, I ask You to bless them, heal them and deliver them. I have been aching for Your fellowship and today I find it as Your friend. I will no longer be controlled by the past, but go forward into the future, trusting You. Cause me to walk as a yielded vessel of forgiveness, holding my identity only in You, that You would be honored. I will no longer be consumed with the destination of my life, but with joy in the journey that You have set before me. Where You lead me, I will follow; where You send me, I will go. Amen.

From Birth to the Burning Bush

Finding and Uprooting the Stronghold of Rejection

CHAPTER 1

The Favor of God

Before Moses, there was God—the Almighty One who craves to bless His creation. He is longing for the fellowship that goes beyond relationship, that conversation of heart that leans into Him and is willing to agree with Him at all costs. He wants to tell us about His majesty and our destiny. Our fellowship with Christ must be about the journey and not the destination, otherwise our disappointments will find a way to manipulate our faith.

In this chapter, before we chase Moses down, we will spend some time discussing the "favor of God." "Why?" you might ask. The reason is because Moses walked in absolute favor with God; he was God's friend. He came to the place where he held nothing higher than the Lord; in fact, nothing else mattered but the Lord; He was enough! We cannot fully understand, nor truly attempt to walk the way Moses did without catching the fundamental truth of how he got there: Moses found a way to agree with God, and so must we! As we progress together, we shall discover that it wasn't always easy for this Egyptian prince who made his home in Midian for so many years. He had to learn how to walk with God, and as we follow him down through the course of time, we too will learn the gait of his step!

God has designed everything so that we could come into communion with Him and walk in agreement and not argument, where the blessings abound. *He desires a trust in our faith, a fellowship in our relationship and an expectancy in our belief.* He has sent the Holy Spirit to move upon us and reside within us to accomplish His will. All of His eternal thoughts focus on how to bless us; it has always been that way, even from the beginning.

> *In the beginning God created the heaven and the earth. And the earth was without form, and void; and darkness was upon the face of the deep. And the spirit of God moved upon the face of the waters. And God said, Let there be light: and there was light* (Genesis 1:1–3).

And so on and so on goes the creation of all things. In chapter 1 of Genesis, we find that "the Spirit of God moved upon the face of the waters." The Holy Spirit moved upon the waters and was waiting for God's command so that He might perform it. When "God said," then it was done! All through this chapter it is noted that God "gave, blessed, saw, created, called, made and said" in a variety of ways for a diversity of purposes. However, it is when God SAID that the Holy Spirit began performing His will. Only when God said did the Holy Spirit begin performing God's will upon the face of the earth. When "God says" over your life and gives the command concerning you, the Holy Spirit moves upon your life as you agree with what God is saying.

Unlike during creation, the Holy Spirit is waiting for man to agree with God. There are times when God speaks creative words that are sovereign when He requires nothing of anyone. But then there are those times when God wants us to come into agreement with Him so that we can come into a place of perfecting, through our partnership with Him in the construction of our soul and character.

The Holy Spirit is ready to move upon your life with great favor as the Lord is proclaiming, "I said" over you! The Holy Spirit is waiting to perform all that God is saying to your soul. Creation groans in front of you, waiting for you to come into agreement with the Lord. Be still with wonder as He whispers to you and stand in amazement as He shouts, "I said!"

Gossip from Hell

There is this thing I call "gossip from hell." *Gossip* is defined by the *Merriam-Webster Dictionary* as a "rumor or report of an intimate nature." Basically it is either a lie or something that is none of our business. The enemy of our soul is good at gossiping. *He will tell us something that hasn't been worked out in heaven yet and convince us to believe a negative report.* Then, if the devil has his way, when heaven makes its announcement in our favor, we have no desire to show up for it.

Many times throughout his career as a human being, Moses listened to gossip from hell, and it cost him clearly. Moses was trapped between wanting to do the right thing and needing to do the wrong thing. He came to the place where he thought his actions would give God's call upon him validity, and instead, they simply created a complication. When Moses saw his near kinsman being mistreated, his passion would become misdirected; and a reaction, instead of a response, would enter his heart. As the wind blew the sand over the body that lay dead at his feet, with blood still on his hands, Moses would know what it feels like when God is not in what you are doing. He would flee to find Him and suffer to know Him. In the end, Moses would learn the value of coming into agreement with God.

Because Moses would listen to the gossip of his unfaithful and ungrateful kinsmen as they shouted lies of his unworthiness while he ran to find God, his search for his Maker would become complicated, frustrated and, to say the least, extended. Their words would be played over in his mind for 40 years, making it almost impossible for him to find and truly know this God he had sworn allegiance to. The words of men would steal his ability to agree with God, so God's favor would be elusive until the day that He would come and find Moses!

One of God's greatest desires is to bless us, but those blessings get blocked when we don't agree with God. In Luke 2:52 the Word says that "Jesus grew in favor with God and man." Even while sweet Calvary was looming off in the distance with its bitter perfume calling in the wind, Jesus was willing at all costs to please His

Father! Hebrews 11 tells us that Enoch had this great testimony: "He pleased God." The "favor" (*charis*, #G5485) in Luke and the "pleased" (*euaresteó*, #G2100) in Hebrews can be connected to the idea of "agreeing" with God. Words with the same meanings are used in the scripture to define Mary, the mother of Jesus; the disciples; Joseph; and King David. Favor came because they agreed with God. When will God's favor have permission to visit you? The favor that God intends to deposit into your life is the same favor that Jesus walked in; it is a divine influence upon someone who is acceptable and pleasing to God.

This past month, when the specialist declared that I had a brain tumor, I had to find God's favor or perfect will in it. I knew the only way that could happen was if I came into agreement with God and not my own fears or the gossiping, lying devil. It felt like I was hearing gossip from the doctor, so I requested another CAT Scan to be scheduled in two days. In those two days I asked God what my reality was. *I had to know if this was gossip from hell or an opportunity of the Lord.* So I went to prayer and asked the Lord for the truth. I told Him, "If this is the dress You bought for me to wear to the party, I will wear it. I don't really like it, and it doesn't seem to fit; but if You bought it, I'll wear it. It's about three sizes too small and orange; I just don't do orange very well. But if You want me to wear it, I shall. We will go to the party, and I will dance with You all night if You want me to. But I have to know that You picked this out for me, then I will submit. If You didn't go shopping, then in Your name, I will peel this pain and disease off me. I just have to know; I must know. I can't make a move until I do because I long to agree with You."

I waited for 35 years to be healed of cystic fibrosis. I'm aware that sometimes people get sick and die; other times they get a miracle and rise up. But there are also those times when there is a process we must walk through, learning to trust the Lord along the way as He builds us. In all these things I have learned that I must never run to my rights, but run to the Lord.

In the gospels, when the widow woman was pounding on the judge's door to be heard, she was screaming to get her way. She was screaming to have her "adversary" removed; not her trouble, but the enemy who was provoking that trouble. We get confused sometimes thinking that just because we have a need, God must answer in our time and our way. That is allowing the need to rule us and not the Lord.

No matter what you are going through, your need might very well be your answer! Jude said to contend for the faith! But we must know what that faith is declaring before we can contend! True faith will desire to live where the favor of God abides, not for the sake of favor, but for the sake of walking in obedience and agreement with God.

Just because you want to believe something, that doesn't make it truth. No matter how many times you shout it out, it isn't truth until God makes it truth. In the midst of my search for truth, the Lord revealed to me (for it was the only revelation that brought peace) that this was just gossip from hell. God's peace is an indicator of God's revelation and truth. If you are unsettled and unsure, choose the way that brings peace to your heart, for surely God resides there. Even if it is something that we don't want to hear, an outfit that we really don't want to wear, if He, the Holy One, is calling us to come, how can we not go that way? It's a level of trust that we must walk in if we expect to ever get out of Midian and conquer Egypt.

Once I had knowledge that the enemy was waging war upon me, the doctor called. I suppose the enemy thought his news would cause me to slide down into a depression covered with despair, but it had the opposite effect. The doctor told me, "These complications are a result of the cystic fibrosis; it has returned." He then began to list all the other symptoms that I could expect (which had already arrived, unknown to him). I hung up the phone, and the Lord brought the devil's worst nightmare upon him. Because I had taken the time to know the truth, I had a "knowing and a peace" and was able to agree with God for whatever His design was.

The Lord asked me, "What do you believe?" I believe the report of the Lord! Sometimes the report of the Lord agrees with the doctor's report; this wasn't one of those times. Since I've had a big chunk of my lung surgically removed, I know what it's like when the Lord agrees with the doctor. But, like I said, this wasn't one of those times! So I shall contend for the faith because I know whom I have believed! I began to tell the enemy to go and commanded the symptoms to go as well. The enemy shouted at me that the pain would increase if I continued, and it did; but I decided that pain never really killed anybody!

Jesus prevailed and within two hours I was totally well. I went in to take another CAT Scan before I caught my flight, and five days later, when I got back home, there was a message on my phone that said, "The CAT Scan is totally normal!"

It's almost like training a dog. You know how when you tell them to "sit and stay," they always try to get up? It's like that! You just have to keep one eye on them to make sure they are behaving themselves. The devil will learn, yes he will. We cannot allow him to steal what the Lord is doing in us. The enemy cannot get us to agree with him when we have chosen to agree with God.

The Power of His Might
"Finally, my brethren, be strong in the Lord, and in the power of his might" (Ephesians 6:10). When this scripture is telling me to "be strong," the meaning is that I have been made able and am empowered.

The power the enemy has holds no authority. God's power, and the power He gives to us, holds all authority for it has dominion over all things. Adam had dominion (or authority) over everything, and he gave it away. The Bible says that things would fear Noah (as he got off the ark), but his dominion over them is not mentioned. We are to take the dominion back from Satan in the name of Jesus by moving in our authority in Christ. We can only do that when we are in agreement with Him.

> *Calvary gives us the power of the blood; the empty tomb gives us the authority to walk in that power!*

If you are at a basketball game, perhaps the player is full of power and ability. Let us say that he is eight feet tall and is a star player, making all the points. The referee is only five feet tall and kind of scrawny, not able to hurt anybody if he had to! Yet despite all of his massive structure, when the star player fouls, the little referee, looking like an insect compared to him, will command him to sit down, and the player will oblige. If he doesn't oblige, his penalty is worse, and eventually he will be thrown out of the game—all because a little referee with no comparable physical power said so! Why? *Because the player had power, but the referee had authority over that power!* We are that referee as we take back the dominion of the devil in the name of Jesus at the prompting of the Holy Spirit.

Calvary gave us the power of the blood; the empty tomb gave us the authority to walk in that power!

The Holy Spirit is ready to move upon you, even after all these years, and He is speaking God's favor and pleasure upon you. Will you agree with Him to receive it? When Moses agreed with God, miracles abounded and promises were realized: a river of favor flowed, a red sea opened. When he disagreed with God, doubt became his companion, and anger was his reward as he led a people who were continually rejecting him.

It would take a lifetime, but Moses would learn the lesson that so many of us refuse to learn, and it is this: No matter what God has called us to do, obedience to Him and not the call is a key to success.

From Favor to Bondage

Before there was Moses, there was the era of favor; this was the time when man's abuses would give way to God's choices. Jacob had 12 sons, and Joseph was one of them. He was living in the original blended family. Dysfunction was the plight of the family that Joseph was born into, but God would prevail and deposit His favor within it because one man rose up and chose to agree with God against the odds.

After years of abuse by his brothers, who were jealous of his father's affection toward him and consideration of him, Joseph found himself at the bottom of a dry well at the hands of his brothers. With the threat of death blowing in the wind, murder gave way to greed, and they sold him as a slave into Egypt. He could have chosen self-pity and hatred, which would have created a poisoning unforgiveness in his heart. But instead, he chose life and walked in forgiveness to see redemption. Because he agreed with God and believed Him when no body else did, an entire nation would bask in the favor of God.

The book of Genesis tells us a story of glory as Joseph went from one trial to the next, refusing to argue with God or disagree with Him. He graduated from one forsaken situation to embrace yet another, all the while daring to believe God was able to turn the evil around him into good. Right in the middle of Joseph's trials and mess, the Word states with unparalleled eloquence time and time again, "And the Lord was with Joseph…." Yet, in all of that, the Bible says that the Word of God came to try Joseph, and try him it did! From the moment he received the vision and the word of how wonderful things were going to be for him, he was a marked man! It happened to Job, to David, to John the Baptist, to me and to you!

As Joseph encouraged his brothers years later in Genesis 50:19–20, "…fear not…for ye thought evil against me; but God meant it unto good, to bring to pass, as it is this day, to save much people alive," we can hear a forgiving heart abound with the health of letting it go. When we agree with God, His favor destroys the evil that would attempt to hold us hostage.

Joseph held the keys to the kingdom, and the king loved Joseph. The Word says that the Israelites were fruitful and increased abundantly and multiplied and waxed exceeding mighty and the land was filled with them. Things are right on track, and then it happened. "Now, there arose up a new king over Egypt, which knew not Joseph" (Exodus 1:8).

> But when the time of the promise drew nigh, which God had sworn to Abraham, the people grew and multiplied in Egypt, til another king arose, which knew not Joseph (Acts 7:17–18).

The new king who did not know Joseph came to town! Isn't that the way it happens? Right when it looks like things might be turning your way, "Wham," the bottom falls out!

How long are you willing to wait for the Lord to show up and rescue you? A day, a decade or a lifetime? When it doesn't matter how long it takes, then you are trusting Him. When you set your mind on the promise—the wait is impossible and full of disappointments; that's when we become at risk of giving our promise away. We need to always set our minds and hearts on the One who gave the promise, and then the new king can never destroy us. When we set our minds and hearts on Christ, it's easy to agree with Him and thereby walk in His favor. The alternative has us walking in confusion and destruction as we agree with the circumstances around us.

God is a better caretaker than our lives generally give Him credit for. The physical things of life often fight the spiritual in an effort to try to prove God wrong; life pushes and shoves, lessons wait and emerge through it as we learn to trust and wait on Him. Unfortunately for the Kingdom of God, "wait" is considered by some of us to be the worst of four-letter words. To wait (*qavah*, #H6960) literally means to "bind together (perhaps by twisting)." We are "twisted up" with Jesus—basically coming into agreement with Him. You can't be braided together or come into partnership with someone whom you don't agree with. Why is agreement so important? Because God wants His favor to be bestowed upon us so we can walk in His blessings!

When the destination has become more powerful than the journey, then we can be tempted to worship the promise and not the One who gave it; favor will never abide there. There are two basic questions that a child will ask while in the backseat of the car on a long journey. 1) When can we stop? and 2) Are we there yet? So it is with us. How many times have we asked, "Lord, when can we stop this, and why aren't we there yet?"

If the waiting has become a torment, then I am in the wrong position in the car. If I'm in the front seat visiting with the driver, enjoying the scenery and music, my drive is less tragic. This is especially true if I'm really interested in having a conversation with the driver. At times like these, the drive can never be too long, and I look forward to it. I'm fellowshipping with someone that I can't get enough of, someone that I look forward to being with, and I cherish every moment.

If you are having a hard time on your journey, get out of the backseat and watch the wonderful change that will take place in your heart and around you! Adjust your position, and your attitude will change.

> *Hast thou not known? Hast thou not heard, that the everlasting God, the Lord, the Creator of the ends of the earth, fainteth not, neither is He weary? There is no searching of his understanding. He giveth power to the faint; and to them that have no might he increaseth strength. Even the youths shall faint and be weary, and the young men shall utterly fall: But they that wait upon the Lord shall renew their strength; they shall mount up with wings as eagles; they shall run, and not be weary; and they shall walk, and not faint* (Isaiah 40:28–31).

One of the most powerful ways to gain strength is to agree with God while you are waiting on Him. Sometimes, it's the *only* way! We learn how to agree with God in the great land of waiting, the place that favor passes through before it comes to us. It has been said that God takes His time to teach us patience!

There should be a great expectancy and anticipation in your soul as you wait upon the Creator of the whole wide universe. As you wait, learn to agree with Him as He makes the march toward you with His powerful favor! May your heart leap as you begin to believe that He has you on His mind, even right now as we race through time to find Moses, the baby boy, being cradled in his mother's arms.

CHAPTER 2

The Goodly Child Knows Rejection

And the woman conceived and bare a son: and when she saw him that he was a goodly child, she hid him three months (Exodus 2:2).

A s we venture backward in time, we find Moses as a baby—a helpless child, the needy one. Before he becomes a man or the vessel of God, before he is the friend of God, he is here in the arms of his mother, Jocabed. He was hidden for three months and ultimately given up to the current of a river.

The Levite tribe was a tribe of dignity and honor. Integrity with great responsibility was at the core of who God designed them to be. These two Levites, Amram and Jocabed, married and produced a goodly child. "Goodly" (*towb*, #H2896) means "good...in the widest sense...best...bountiful, cheerful...joyful, kindly...merry...pleasant...precious, prosperity...wealth...well (-favored)." And, we can see by scripture that they had no fear of the king's commandment.

By faith Moses, when he was born, was hid three months of his parents, because they saw he was a proper [goodly] child; and they were not afraid of the king's commandment (Hebrews 11:23).

It must have been a very difficult thing to hide a baby for three months. Babies cry. Babies laugh. Babies make weird noises and give off funny smells. Sometimes babies scream, even if they are "goodly." Babies are hard to hide, especially for three months! But it doesn't appear that the parents had much fear of anything except God. When you have a healthy respect for God, you will be provoked to do amazing things for His honor.

His parents must have been rare—defending the honor of God upon their child and recognizing his calling before he could even speak. They operated on a level of love that had no fear. If they hadn't, it would have been difficult to hide that child as long as they did and then abandon him to the rushing river's water.

> **When you have a healthy respect for God, you will be**
> **provoked to do amazing things for His honor.**

History never records that Moses was ever circumcised. In fact, it says at one point that he was not circumcised. His parents went beyond the law and moved into love. How could this child survive in Egypt if he was circumcised? They believed the promise and forsook the traditions that would attempt to offend that promise. Are your own traditions offending the promise of God that you are desperately trying to believe?

In Egypt, the Israelites were slaves working with brick and mortar, but their spirits were unquenchable, even as the king's insecurity turned to fear. The king must have been somewhat of an historian because he was concerned about Israel rising up and becoming a nation. He knew it had been prophesied centuries earlier that a man would be born to lead them out of Egypt, and he was paying attention! The king knew the time was at hand for Israel to move beyond Egypt, and that knowledge led him to violence.

The king commanded the midwives to kill all the Hebrew boys who were born. But the midwives disobey the order because they feared God. When the king asked why they had disobeyed him, they said, "Because the Hebrew women are not as the Egyptian women; for they are lively, and are delivered ere the midwives come in unto them" (Exodus 1:19). The king couldn't stop these women, so he became angry. He declared to the people that they could keep the baby girls, but the boy babies had to be thrown into the river. And, to the river Moses eventually went. But not at the king's command—at God's command, for God had a plan. Moses was taken to the river when God said it was time and not a minute sooner.

The vehicle that Moses occupied as he waited for the provision of God was a little basket or ark, which his mother carefully made. His journey down the river was supervised under the watchful eye of his sister, Miriam. The Pharaoh's daughter, who was down by the river, saw the basket and the crying baby in it. She took the baby and noticed that he was a Hebrew child. Suddenly, Miriam appeared. She offered to find a Hebrew woman to nurse the child for her. The Pharaoh's daughter agreed and even offered to pay the Hebrew woman to care for this child until it was weaned. Jocabed was that woman.

Amram and Jocabed persevered to provide for the promise of God in their child. When Pharaoh was trying to kill the hope of Israel, they were rocking him. A parent has a powerful privilege and duty to help a child realize that they can, indeed, rule the world if they wish.

> And the child grew, and she [Jocabed] brought him unto Pharaoh's daughter, and he became her son. And she called his name Moses; and she said, Because I drew him out of the water (Exodus 2:10).

Scripture tells us "and he became her son...." Such a painful statement for Amram and Jocabed. Their beloved son, whom they birthed, loved and taught, became the son of another! When he cried, they were there; when he had victories, they were there. All those nights of watching him sleep and seeing his goodness abound during the day had abruptly ended.

Psychologists tell us that a child's emotional stability or instability is established by the time they are five years old—and sometimes even younger. Moses was being raised for success. But could that "raising" set him on the right path for his lifetime, even in the house of Pharaoh?

We have to believe that Moses received some of his parents' boldness because they trained him and taught him for Pharaoh's daughter until he was weaned, which could have taken up to five years. What a powerful time of influence the Lord allowed Amram and Jocabed to have! I am convinced that they did not waste those early years with Moses.

In time, when Jocabed delivered her son into the hands of the oppressors, Moses found himself adopted, apparently abandoned by those who had loved and cared for him all his years. Suddenly things changed. He was now to be raised by the oppressor of his people, the heathen king. In the years to come, Moses would have to decide if this man, Pharaoh, was to be a distant shadow or a reckoning force in his life.

Did Moses feel orphaned? And did those feelings worm their way into his heart and cause him to believe a lie and become confused? So much of the time we are not truly rejected, abandoned or orphaned. The devil just makes us think we are so that we cannot advance against his kingdom (more gossip from hell). The prince of darkness has no ethics. It is easy to hear the enemy shouting at us when we are being pulled by momentary emotion. Perhaps Moses wondered if he did something wrong. "Is that why I have to leave?" he may have asked himself. So many questions went unanswered; and most of them fostered guilt, rejection and insecurity, not to mention feelings of abandonment.

Perhaps during the previous year Moses had been told what was going to eventually happen to him. Perhaps he knew. No matter what he knew or didn't know, this one grinding truth was inescapable: he was only a kid, a mere child who was being forced to leave his brother, sister, mother and father. Sweet, lonely, goodly boy.

It would be difficult to allow your infant to float down the current of a river. It would be harder still to let him float over to the enemy's camp and into the arms of your torturer. But Moses's parents did.

They had no fear, for they were trusting in the God who had given them a mighty promise.

At an age when most mothers are marching their children off to preschool or kindergarten, Jocabed had to take her son to his new "family." I wonder what she and Amram had originally named Moses, and I wonder if they hoped this day would never come. Perhaps they had convinced themselves Pharaoh's daughter would change her mind and not ask for their son. Maybe, they might have hoped, it was just a fleeting idea to her. The empty hole it would leave in their hearts and house must have been larger than life.

He became the grandson of the heathen ruler that had made a life's occupation out of beating his people and using them as slaves. His mother was forced to bring the evil king a gift of a goodly child. Her son was now heir to the fortune and folly of Egypt. When it was time, when the waiting was over, when this little one was a man, would he hear God? And would he obey? Surely, God Himself would have to intervene in the years to come if this new prince of Egypt was to follow God's ways. This was not a job for a mere man; it would take a supernatural God.

So Moses goes from mother to mother. The cry of the one leaving him and the joy of the one embracing him would no doubt leave a pain in his heart. So many children at that age don't want to leave their parents. Was Moses that way? Did he cry and scream as his mother left, or was he heartbreakingly brave? The rejection that he must have felt, the loneliness and fear that gripped his heart, no doubt kept him company for many years. We see these struggles with feelings of rejection later in his desert experience. Oh, the tragedy of tragedy forming us!

The food of his new home was entirely different. The music had to bring pain to his ears, and the language more than likely offended his little heart. The customs were not only different, they were probably the exact opposite of what he was used to. The son of Amram and Jocabed would have to learn his new name and shed all hope of ever returning to the arms of his real mother. He had just been given up for adoption and had to overcome that pain. His identity was stripped away, and he spent the next 80 years trying to find it again.

He was adopted not as a slave, but as a prince, which held a greater requirement to conform to the ways of the one who adopted him. He found himself very much alone, without a friend in the world, a mere baby in a land full of evil, lonely and misunderstood.

Moses left the joy of the Levite home to be part of a hard-driving, prideful people. The Word of God says that Moses was well trained by the Egyptians. Did he measure up? Perhaps he wasn't any good at driving a chariot or sitting on thrones or delegating authority around the palace. Maybe he didn't possess princely attributes because he was not truly an Egyptian. Was he persecuted and told that he would never be good enough?

Or perhaps Moses was quite good at every task that was presented to him. Maybe he became an expert in all that was set before him to do. Perhaps he was accomplished. If this is the case, then there was a different set of circumstances that he had to deal with—perhaps worse. These would shout to him that he was great and capable. Pride and arrogance would be introduced to him and when it came, it would find a place to produce the offspring of his hidden anger.

BEING great is different from KNOWING that you are! When you know it, the information can handicap you when your destination is to reside in the palm of God's hand.

Whether Moses was good at being well trained or not is almost irrelevant because the persecution for who he was, and who he was attempting to become as he left the people of mud and straw for the palace, must have been a force in his life. It was a force that I believe provoked his heart to gain a flaw in all his greatness. His greatness was accompanied by an arrogance that was continually trying to cover up his pain—the pain of rejection.

The Spirit of Rejection

Their son, the goodly child, the one they saw the favor of God upon so many years earlier, was not only being raised and instructed by the Egyptians, their persecutors, but he was being *well trained* by them. The spirit of rejection hovered over Moses, fighting with the Holy Spirit for the position in the heart of this boy who had no home. The day that Moses was given away, the fertile soil of his soul was opened up and the seed of rejection was deposited into a place that would, if given the right set of circumstances, develop a root that would flourish in the crevices of his spirit. The root of rejection is able to become a spiritual stronghold that will cause the deepest of men and the most chosen of women to crumble under its power.

Amram and Jocabed had to give up who they loved and allow him to be touched by something and someone that they despised. No matter how it appeared over the next few decades, they had to believe that God would redeem all of it. Oh, how they must have wanted to intervene and "help" the situation turn toward God. But I believe they knew and understood the power of prayer, so they persevered in it.

Amram and Jocabed gave Moses up for the cause of God. And, as the years would roll by, they had to hold onto the belief that, no matter how it looked, God was going to be faithful to their obedience. Trusting the Lord took on an entirely new meaning when they let go of their son that day. Because of their obedience, the deliverance of their people would come!

Faith is knowing something will come to pass; trust is not caring how or when it will.

I remember when my son was in high school, and he decided that his truck was a great toy to have—a very fast toy, mind you. He was redecorating the roads with the rubber from his tires. One day, while I was lecturing him about it, a friend happened to stop by and said, "What are you so bothered about? He's a good kid. He's just sowing some wild oats!" I stood to my feet and angrily shouted at her, "I am not raising a bowl of oatmeal, I am raising a man!" (And he is a wonderful man of God today.)

In the end, the Lord will prevail, for Isaiah 54:17 says that no weapon formed against me will prosper. No weapon, not even oatmeal! Amram and Jocabed believed God would take care of what they had entrusted to Him. They made a decision to trust God and forced themselves to live by that decision.

Nobody can raise the white flag that flies over your life but you. Does that flag shout "surrender" to the Lord or to the Liar? May we raise the standards in our lives to reflect the decisions we have made for God.

CHAPTER 3

Death by Choice

Being "called" or "chosen" is a matter of choice—not God's, but ours. In order to choose life, as Paul said, we must choose God's ways above our own! As we submit to God's design, we yield to God's perfection in us and emerge as trusted vessels, fit for His use. As we take on the likeness of Christ, day by day, we begin to automatically respond as He would, because we are becoming one with Him.

This man from the Levite tribe, born to Amram and Jocabed at a critical time in history, went from preparation for his purpose to losing his identity so that he could receive the favor of a face-to-face fellowship with the living God. He would eventually see the Red Sea parted, battles supernaturally won, the earth opened up to devour his accusers, bread falling from heaven, birds piled up to be roasted, water coming out of rocks and would be given a compass that was a pillar of fire by night and a pillar of cloud by day.

Moses is one of the best-known characters in the Old Testament, yet he was also one of the frailest and most insecure of men. We have heard of the power that hovered over Moses. Many of us visualize all the great manifestations of God's faithfulness to him. I'm less interested in the miracles than I am the reason that they came. Yes, they came for the people, but what of the man who carried them?

How did he get to the place where God said He would talk to him face-to-face? How did he get to the place where it was noted that God showed His "ways" to Moses, but only His "acts" to the Israelites? How did he get to the place where the favor of God was upon him, the power of God went before him and the protection of God kept his back safe? How did this man, who carried both the scars of childhood rejection and insecurity, along with the abilities of an Egyptian prince, get there? How did a man from Midian ever walk as a choice vessel of God? And, can we? Sometimes our wounds and memories are just too much to bear. It's hard to imagine that the Lord could cause anything great to come from them or through them. Yet, Isaiah 61:3 tenderly whispers that God will give us "beauty for ashes, the oil of joy for mourning, the garment of praise for the spirit of heaviness; that they might be called trees of righteousness, the planting of the LORD, that he might be glorified."

This man from Midian, who was on a crash course with God Himself, could not have known fully what the future would hold. He came to a place where 40 years of living, teaching and training became his enemy. He had to find a way to forsake all that he knew to embrace, that which was foreign to him. God was a stranger to him, and it would be in this strange land that he would meet Him.

Moses and his God went from pushing and pulling to walking and trusting. As we go forward in pursuing the life of Moses, we will come to understand this element of their fellowship above all others: Moses would have to continually yield who he was to who God is.

Called or Chosen?

> *But ye are a chosen generation, a royal priesthood, an holy nation, a peculiar people; that ye should shew forth the praises of him who hath called you out of darkness into his marvellous light* (1 Peter 2:9).

There are two words in this passage that I want to discuss: "called" and "chosen." These two words have their root meanings found in Matthew 20:16, "So, the last shall be first, and the first last; for many be called but few chosen." To be called is to be invited or appointed.

To be chosen is to *accept* the invitation or appointment; not to have *been* the choice, but to have *made* the choice. It is choosing to die in order to make the choice. It is to prefer the choice you have made over all other things and to submit to divine selection within it. No matter who we are, the option is ours. We choose to be "called" or we choose to be "chosen," but we are the ones who choose.

Even if we were never "given away" as a child physically, many of us feel as if we have been. Often this sense of abandonment tries to mold us and causes us to be desperate hostages to the "called lifestyle," while the choice to be chosen seems to linger far off.

So we find out that almost everyone is invited, but only a few accept the invitation. It isn't that God says, "I chose only this one because he/she is my favorite." He is saying, "Y'all come!" Some will and some won't. What is "coming"? It is agreeing with God, walking in a partnership with Him, accepting His invitation for fellowship, choosing Him above all others and submitting to Him. It is choosing Christ in the deepest sense. When you do, you begin to walk in the favor of God as a chosen vessel of honor. Not because He supernaturally made you do it, but because you decided to take Him up on His offer!

Paul told Timothy that, "In a great house there are not only vessels of gold and of silver, but also of wood and of earth; and some to honour, and some to dishonour" (2 Tim. 2:20). This is the difference between behaving as one chosen or one called.

Paul was not speaking of the unsaved, but the saved. Dishonorable servants of God, those who refuse to be chosen, find a way to be content with being called.

Enoch only preached one sermon that we know of (see Jude 14–16), and in it he comes against the "ungodly godly people." He could have come against any type of person in his "one shot," but what he did was tell the people of God to start acting like the people of God. Basically he was saying, "Behave as one chosen!"

Isaiah 48 says that the Lord has chosen us out of the fire of affliction. Chosen people will go through the fire! Called people will walk around it and talk about how warm it is and how beautiful it is, even how dangerous it is; but they will never truly experience it, because they don't choose to. They are in the way. The qualification for the favor of God, on the other hand, is a willingness to be made excellent in agreement with God. The "chosen" (*bachar*, #H977) in Isaiah 48 literally means "to try" and be made "excellent."

In order to agree with God, we have to be willing to be wrong.

Hebrews 12 tells us that we are corrected by God because it profits us and allows us to partake of God's own holiness. In order to agree with God, we have to be willing to be wrong.

When Moses was willing to be wrong, his world began to open up to him. When Moses was willing to be misunderstood, he began to walk as a chosen vessel of God. For many years he had received his identity from what had happened to him and not by whom God had chosen him to be!

It was only after the Damascus Road experience in Acts 9:15 that the Lord tells Ananias that Paul is a "chosen vessel unto Me." This came after Paul submitted to the Lord, lost himself in blindness and agreed with God. Then, by his actions, he declared he would forsake the "called" status that normal people occupy and walk in the "chosen state" of those who only want the Lord. He was willing to be peculiar. He never looked back because the favor of God is a forward force.

Hebrews 11:24–26 says that

> *Moses...refused to be called the son of Pharaoh's daughter; Choosing rather to suffer affliction with the people of God, than to enjoy the pleasures of sin for a season; Esteeming the reproach of Christ greater riches than the treasures in Egypt; for he had respect unto the recompence of the reward.*

The man's life was a definite series of choices. It appears that he had his eye on the mark of the prize of the high calling. He was after obedience, and it required a choice. "Choosing" here in Hebrews still means to have chosen deliberately and without thought of consequences.

Our ability to assume what God wants can cost us 40 years of wandering in the desert. I believe Moses agreed with God back in Egypt, but then he got confused about what that agreement meant. You'll always make a mistake when you do that. His murder of the Egyptian didn't change his destiny; it just complicated it. Poor Moses—all that passion and no direction.

Moses sensed what he was supposed to do, but his belief about how that would happen created trials and tribulations in his life. The Egyptian error cost him plenty. When we turn from obedience, it isn't so much that we are turning from God; it's that we are turning toward ourselves. And often, it's a trap of the enemy to cause an unfavorable consequence to rest upon us.

In 1577 Sir Francis Drake wrote the following poem as he submitted himself to God's will and attempted to destroy any selfish desires in his heart:

> Disturb us, Lord, when
> We are too well pleased with ourselves,
> When our dreams have come true
> Because we've dreamed too little,
> When we arrived safely
> Because we've sailed too close to the shore.
>
> Disturb us, Lord, when
> With the abundance of things we possess
> We have lost our thirst
> For the waters of life;
> Having fallen in love with life,
> We have ceased to dream of eternity
> And in our efforts to build a new earth,
> We have allowed our vision
> Of the new Heaven to dim.
>
> Disturb us, Lord, to dare more boldly,
> To venture on wider seas
> Where storms will show your mastery;

Where losing sight of land,
We shall find the stars.

We ask you to push back
The horizons of our hopes;
And to push into the future
In strength, courage, hope and love.

Sir Francis Drake understood some things. He understood about not only choosing Christ above himself, but about choosing Christ above himself and all others. When we get it through our heads that to choose Christ means that we have not chosen ourselves, and not even Him, but His fullness, then the rules change. If you know what it means to choose Christ, you protect that choice, and you do so because that choice has come at a high cost. To choose Christ is a privilege that many of us just walk past because of cost or inconvenience. Once you have decided that's what you are going to do, though, the options surrounding that decision fade away because when something is written in stone, it is written. It's no longer an idea!

Today, as you ponder the prospect of walking as a chosen vessel of God, may you move past the strongholds that have prevented it before. No matter how guilty you are, whom you have hurt or how rejected you have felt, those things don't have to call your name anymore. Moses recovered, and so can you!

CHAPTER 4

Pride Confuses the Choosing

And it came to pass in those days, when Moses was grown, that he went out unto his brethren, and looked on their burdens: and he spied an Egyptian smiting an Hebrew, one of his brethren. And he looked this way and that way, and when he saw that there was no man, he slew the Egyptian, and hid him in the sand. And when he went out the second day, behold, two men of the Hebrews strove together and he said to him that did the wrong, Wherefore smitest thou thy fellow? And he said, Who made thee a prince and a judge over us? Intendest thou to kill me as thou killedst the Egyptian? And Moses feared and said, Surely this thing is known. Now when Pharaoh heard this thing, he sought to slay Moses. But, Moses fled from the face of Pharaoh and dwelt in the land of Midian; and he sat down by a well (Exodus 2:11–15).

One of the definitions of "fear" (*yare*, #H3372) in the above verses means to "reverence," which really puts a twist on things for me. Earlier I had believed that Moses ran because he was afraid of the Egyptians or his kinsman who was shouting at him before he left. Yes, the words jumped in his heart, but they wouldn't emerge until later. He actually left because he realized that God wasn't the one moving through his hands as he killed the Egyptian. He fled because he knew, in that instant, that he really didn't know God; all he had was an idea of God. In reality, Moses was saying, "Great, I've just discovered that I'm not 'all that.' I have gotten ahead of God! I told the mountain to move, and the whole world is watching and the mountain hasn't even flinched." The revelation of who he was hit him. He was abundantly aware of the fact that he had jumped in the middle of his calling, and God didn't jump when he said to! Moses knew now, without a doubt, that he would continue to fail in his quest unless he could learn to go with God and not himself!

There is a little less liability when you face an Egyptian on your own than when you face Pharaoh on your own. Moses is forced to face the fact that he has a great idea, but his presentation stinks. When Pharaoh sought to kill him, he knew that he was on his own, for God was waiting for him in Midian. He needed to go and find this God who was reaching out to him from across the desert sand.

It wasn't until later, when Moses realized the wind was out of his sails, so to speak, and he was stranded in a little boat, alone in the middle of a vast ocean with raging, emotional waves all around him, that he remembered, "Oh yeah, this is God's deal—only He is strong enough!" He didn't run in fear of the king—that wasn't in him—but he ran in reverence of God. "What have I done?" he wondered. He must have realized, "There is no safety net on this thing. It's either God or it isn't, but I'm not part of the equation!" His search for the reverence of God began that day as he realized that although God didn't need him, God wanted him. His pride had stripped him of the power of God in his life and insisted that he choose his own ways above God's ways.

Moses was full of wisdom and courage, as Acts 7:22 says: "Moses was learned in all the wisdom of the Egyptians, and was mighty in words and in deeds." Moses was full of confidence and passion for what he was about to do. When we have the "what" down, we still need to wait for the "how" and "when." Those things are hidden within the revelation of who God is. He is the "who." Moses had been trained for almost four decades as the great prince of Egypt.

There were few who could measure up, I'm sure. He wasn't just good, he was mighty. There were few things that were not within his grasp. But soon, his position would be like sand sliding through his fingers.

When we begin to place the greatness of who we are above the greatness of what we are chosen by God to do, it all goes bad. When Moses did that, he began to touch the "why" of the thing, which is something that is strictly God's business. Only He is eternal and all-knowing.

The same thing happened to Jonah, then he found the belly of the whale. The same thing happened to Jacob until he found Laban's camp. The same thing happened to Samson when he thought his destiny would be fulfilled in the camp of the Philistines. And then there is Judas, the man with a plan. Jehu came and put a little too much of who he was into what he was doing for the Lord. When you do that, you quit leaning on God and learning from Him. Has the same thing happened to you?

The difference between an empowering and limiting action is the difference between living in God's wisdom or following our own foolishness.

You can have desire and no gifting. You can be gifted and not called. (See 1 Corinthians 12.) You can be called and not anointed. You can be anointed and not ordained. You can be ordained and not appointed. It is God who brings balance and makes it work. Just because we're gifted doesn't mean we're called to do anything with our gifts at that moment. Sometimes we aren't supposed to bless everyone with our giftings! For example, I can make a pretty good pie. But that doesn't mean I'm supposed to set everything aside and open a bakery. It means I'm supposed to be a preacher who can make a pie. As we wait upon God, He will present all the gifting, calling, anointing, appointing, validation, affirmation and ordination we need to fulfill the desire of His heart in us.

Getting ahead of God
The story of Cushi and Ahimaaz in the Old Testament is a great example of somebody getting ahead of God.

Then said Ahimaaz the son of Zadok, Let me now run, and bear the king tidings, how that the Lord hath avenged him of his enemies. And Joab said unto him, Thou shalt not bear tidings this day, but thou shalt bear tidings another day: but this day thou shalt bear no tidings, because the king's son is dead. Then said Joab to Cushi, Go tell the king what thou hast seen. And Cushi bowed himself unto Joab, and ran. Then said Ahimaaz the son of Zadok yet again to Joab, But howsoever, let me, I pray thee, also run after Cushi. And Joab said, Wherefore wilt thou run, my son, seeing that thou hast no tidings ready? But howsoever, said he, let me run. And he said unto him, Run. Then Ahimaaz ran by the way of the plain, and overran Cushi. And David sat between the two gates: and the watchman went up to the roof over the gate unto the wall, and lifted up his eyes, and looked, and behold a man running alone. And the watchman cried, and told the king. And the king said, If he be alone, there is tidings in his mouth. And he came apace, and drew near.

And the watchman saw another man running: and the watchman called unto the porter, and said, Behold another man running alone. And the king said, He also bringeth tidings. And the watchman said, Me thinketh the running of the foremost is like the running of Ahimaaz the son of Zadok. And the king said, He is a good man, and cometh with good tidings. And Ahimaaz called, and said unto the king, All is well. And he fell down to the earth upon his face before the king, and said, Blessed be the Lord thy God, which hath delivered up the men that lifted up their hand against my lord the king. And the king said, Is the young man Absalom safe? And Ahimaaz answered, When Joab sent the king's servant, and me thy servant, I saw a great tumult, but I knew not what it was. And the king said unto him, Turn aside, and stand here. And he turned aside, and stood still.

And, behold, Cushi came; and Cushi said, Tidings, my lord the king: for the Lord hath avenged thee this day of all them that rose up against thee. And the king said unto Cushi, Is the young man Absalom safe? And Gushi answered, The enemies of my lord the king, and all that rise against thee to do thee hurt, be as that young man is. And the king was much moved, and went up to the chamber over the gate, and wept: and as he went, thus he said, O my son Absalom, my son, my son Absalom! would God I had died for thee, O Absalom, my son, my son! (2 Samuel 18:19–33)

Cushi had the gift and the purpose. Ahimaaz had only the gift. Pride and confidence in his own ability made him go forward into a work that was not his own. Ahimaaz ran without a vision or a call. There was a purpose for the running, but clearly, he didn't own it. Be careful when you start confusing your revelation with God's revelation; they are not the same. A need does not automatically present you with a calling to fulfill that need. You may possess the gift, but without the calling to perform it, you can create problems.

Ahimaaz was not ordained by God or appointed by anyone around him. He was commissioned while he was looking in the mirror. He could run, and he knew it. But he misunderstood the mission; it was never about running, it was about how you would handle yourself when you were done running! Ahimaaz heard of the mission and literally begged General Joab to send him. He was told no. Ahimaaz persevered through spoiled impatience and began driving Joab crazy, so Joab caved in and told him to go—but not until after Cushi had already left on his journey. Joab sent the right man for the job, and Ahimaaz couldn't stand it; pride will do that.

Moses, the prince of Egypt, was sure of who he was, too, until he got a revelation of his own inability. Ahimaaz was so consumed with his own talent that he couldn't walk in God's revelation.

**God wants our obedience
more than our sacrifice, service and talent.**

The scripture says it looked like the running of Ahimaaz. Apparently, this guy was a famous runner. People would see him from far away, and recognize his style of running. Ahimaaz was a gifted runner; he knew it, and so did many people around him. Yet Joab never asked him to run. God wants our obedience more than our sacrifice, service and talent.

In fact, Ahimaaz was such a great runner that he actually ran right past Cushi on the way to the king's place. Too bad it wasn't about the running—he could have won a prize! Ahimaaz arrived first and spoke an incomplete truth to the king, accompanied by an inappropriate presentation. He had a story without any experience, and was told to turn aside and stand in a corner. Basically, he was chastised and told to go stand in the corner. I suppose the revelation of his self-imposed identity is revealed as he heads toward the wall because he not only stands in the corner, but the Word says he was very still doing it. It's always hard to find out that you have been an idiot when everyone else is finding it out too! When our self-importance is on display, it is a little harder to destroy. Nevertheless, this is what God requires in order for us to become fit vessels.

Ahimaaz stood in a corner discovering truth that doesn't mention his name, only God's. Cushi came bearing the gift, as well as the calling, to accomplish the task at hand. The grace with which he handled himself with the king is proof that he was the right choice. Never underestimate the running shoes of a man with a mandate from God!

The Lord has to add the power to our process. He will only do that when the time is right and when we've been made ready. Of course, me thinking I'm ready and God thinking I'm ready are two very different things.

The Desert Experience
Once the revelation that he could not continue in his own strength hit him, Moses gained a reverence for God that left no room to revere himself. That reverence caused him to flee. At some point, we all must go back to the first revelation (the one that Adam had): "Behold, I am made of dirt!" Moses is faced with the prospect of

being the "dirt king," and nothing more. He would struggle with this up until the day when his hidden identity would meet a rock in the desert of Zin and he would be rescued from himself.

Moses went to the desert for 40 years to destroy who he was and find out who God was. Galatians says that Paul was in the Arabian desert for three years. We do not know how long John the Baptist was in the wilderness with the locusts; one day he just emerged. The "setting aside" for Paul and John moved them past being mere men and into the state where honored vessels live.

Moses fled from his own country, and then a strange thing happened. "But Moses fled from the face of Pharaoh, and dwelt in the land of Midian: and he sat down by a well" (Exodus 2:15). He became a stranger in this new land of Midian; and although he didn't know it, his heart was preparing to endure some of the most lonely, frustrating and depressing times he would have since saying goodbye to his mother.

Moses no longer had the confidence of being the prince of Egypt. He ran from who he was in an attempt to run to God. In order to find Him, he would have to venture through the turmoils of life to wind up on holy ground. Sometimes while we are traveling through the deserts of life, we need to believe that there is a cause that beats tending sheep. Moses would find that cause on a mountain that was provoking him to come closer. That's why he went to Midian in the first place, to find God. Midian was where the Mountain of God, Mount Horeb, emerged out of the ground as a monument to God. He ran to the right place for the right reason, but when he arrived, he forgot why he went.

Tending sheep in Midian was a strange occupation for this man from Egypt. What was he doing sitting down by a well when he had Israel on his mind, anyway? What are we doing sitting down by a well? Sitting by a well is like mindless entertainment. That's what people do when they don't know what to do. As we shall see, Moses became depressed and, quite literally, sat down. He was supposed to be getting ready to be made ready. How long is it supposed to take? Did it have to take 40 years for him to make the right choice? Or perhaps Moses just wasn't a very good student. There is a good chance that he wasn't working at it very hard. There are people who like to talk about what they are going to do but are unwilling to pay the price, and so they never do anything. Moses had become one of these people during his tour of Midian. Some of us are so afraid of being wrong that we never venture out to let God make us right!

Letting go of who we are and the greatness of who we have become can take a moment or a lifetime. For Moses, his struggle took 40 years. He was eventually ready to see the burning bush, or God wouldn't have presented it; but ready and willing can be worlds apart. I can't help but think that Moses wasn't working at it all that hard. Did he become one of the "someday" people? "I'm going to do this...someday!" In the meantime, the world passes them by because they just can't get up off the side of the well.

Take a look at this story I once heard:

> Bob and Charlie started working for the railroad on the same day—in fact, the same hour—and they were hired to do the same job. Twenty years later, Bob was still "working the line" with all the other men when the executive train pulled up. A well-dressed man got out of the train and started asking if anyone knew where Bob was. He had heard he was working the line on that part of the track, doing maintenance. Yes, Bob was there. Everyone directed the man toward Bob and, as he approached, both men smiled. Bob wiped his hands off carefully, shook the other man's hand, and said, "Well, how ya' doing, Charlie? It's been a while!" The men visited for a few moments and then Charlie had to leave. Charlie waved to Bob as the train pulled away, and Bob tipped his hat.
>
> The other workers could not understand why this man, who was the president of the railway, had come to see Bob, or how Bob knew the president in the first place. Bob told them, "We started working for the railroad on the same day, at the same hour. In fact, Charlie used to work this exact line with me many years ago."

Most of the men nodded and walked away, except for one man. He stayed and asked the question that defines human nature: "If you both started working for the railroad at the same time and did the same work, then how come you are still doing the same job 20 years later, and Charlie is now the president?"

Bob stood up and answered, "Oh, that's easy. You see, 20 years ago, I just went to work. But Charlie? He went to work for the railroad!"

So, who are you working for?

It's tough to move when you get comfortable, isn't it? It's not like sitting down is necessarily wrong; but when you are advancing in the Kingdom of God and attempting to destroy the enemy's strongholds, sitting down probably isn't the best weapon of choice. So, examine what you are doing and consider if it's what God wants. Have you just been running like Ahimaaz because you can? Perhaps you are hiding in those running shoes from who you know deep down the Lord has destined you to be.

Sometimes it's hard to lay our pride down because we can't find it. It's buried too deeply within ourselves, hiding. But to become a vessel of God, we must root it out and give God a clean canvas to paint His masterpiece upon. We can't depend upon the paint that life has thrown on our canvas, but only what God will put there—and we have to trust Him for that!

God was trying to make the man able in Him, that's what vessels are made of—God's ability. Moses was stuck for 40 years between a calling and a choice. His manhood would have to give way to his God.

"I would have fainted, unless I had believed to see the goodness of the Lord in the land of the living" (Psalm 27:13). Just believe God is with you—because He is!

CHAPTER 5

Rejecting Words

L et us venture back to Egypt once again to the murder scene. I want to show you something. "And (Moses) was told, Who made thee a prince and a judge over us? Do you intend to kill me as you killed the Egyptian?" (Exodus 2:14)

As Moses went forward, causing his misunderstanding of direction to become his reality, someone came against him. This was a critical point of change for Moses. He seemed to be fine until somebody spoke up. It doesn't appear that Moses had any second thoughts about what he'd done until this person confronted him. He had just murdered someone, yet there is no hint of insecurity on his part until that moment. I would think Moses would be feeling upset or fearful, but the Word is clear that he was not afraid.

Because Moses was consumed with what he was doing, he wasn't free to pursue God; he had to collect a little insecurity along the way. Wounds never like to be alone. When you minister out of your own hurt, you will always attract wounds, and your gifts cannot be trusted. This is why Jesus said in John, "The devil has come and he has no part of me." The Lord was speaking about the care He had taken with His soul. The devil couldn't touch Him. Jesus had no unattended wounds that were oozing poison into His soul.

It's the same care we are instructed to take in Ephesians 6, when the Word instructs us to put on the whole armor of God. It must be put on to be effective. Does your armor fit or is it clanging around ineffectively? We have to practice giving our pain to the Lord; and then, after a while, it will become an automatic response. To operate as a vessel of God, Moses would have to learn that healed people heal and wounded people wound. It doesn't get any simpler than that!

The Lord said that He suffered in all ways like we did. When He told Paul in 2 Corinthians 12:9, "My grace is sufficient for thee," He was saying, "Hey, I did it so that you can do it in Me." "Grace" refers to our inherited right and our ability in Christ. Grace is both proactive and interactive. God designed it that way. Grace accommodates our ability to choose. Remember, it is our inherited right to be chosen and not merely called.

The devil couldn't find a chink in the Lord's armor. No holes and no dents. As much as the enemy lingered like a vapor, debating with the Holy Spirit for the will of Jesus, he could never win because Jesus's armor was intact—no wounds, no holes, no limps, no scars. A perfect lamb!

If Moses had been confident in who God was in him, he could have simply admitted that he'd made a mistake and gotten out of step with God, repented of overdressing, and regained the reverence for God that he needed. This could have happened in a moment. But instead, on the way to gain the reverence he lacked for God, he left for Midian with a bag of emotional terror brought on by rejection. He began organizing his garbage instead of getting rid of it. His rejection issue was separate from his lack of reverence, and it rose up to complicate the cure. Then the armor makes a sound, "ca-chink!"

The Words of Others
Because he was more concerned with his own identity than God's, Moses had confidence only in who he was in God—not in who God was in him. The difference cost him a few decades. The words of an angry person watered the seed of rejection that was hidden deep in his soul. Watered seeds produce roots; familiar spirits and strongholds will attach themselves to those roots in an attempt to control our lives.

Moses had confidence only in who he was in God—
not in who God was in him.

The words of another person paralyzed his ability to move in his calling. The words of another stole 40 years from him. Those words shouted, "Who made thee a prince and a judge over us? Do you intend to kill me as you killed the Egyptian?" It was only after these words were uttered that Moses fled from the face of Pharaoh and dwelt in the land of Midian to sit down by a well. Moses became insecure after he paid attention to the words of those who did not understand his actions or his destiny. The spirit of rejection was able to take root and flourish under the watchful care of men's words.

The same thing happened to Elijah when he found the cave, to Lot when he lost his voice in Sodom, to Hezekiah when he made the Babylonians lunch. And the same thing happens every day to people who want to be Shadrach, Meshach and Abednego, but are so afraid of the fire and insecure about who God is in them that they simply bow before the idol and pretend they are tying their shoes.

The spirit of rejection will cause you to operate your life from either the platform of protection or performance. You will either avoid situations that would provoke you to launch out into the deep, in order to protect your heart from feeling pain, or you will find a place of acceptance and be content there so that you are not at risk of pain or failure.

Moses was a man without a country. The Egyptians were seeking to kill him, and his kinsmen had judged him unworthy. This journey was the beginning of his refining that would lead to the uprooting of the spirit of rejection as he was driven into Midian. Still, he believed that God had something for him to do, because Acts 7:23–25 says,

> *And when he was full forty years old, it came into his*
> *heart to visit his brethren, the children of Israel. And*
> *seeing one of them suffer wrong, he defended him, and*

avenged him that was oppressed and smote the Egyptian: For he supposed his brethren would have understood how that God by his hand would deliver them: but they understood it not.

We must never allow the reactions of other people to either validate or destroy our passion for what the Lord has set in our hearts to do. Clearly, what Moses did was wrong. Murder as a means to obeying God isn't all that great of a tribute to obedience! Nevertheless, the people's words shouldn't have discouraged him from choosing God's design. If someone else understands your destiny, it doesn't make it valid. It may make it easier, but not valid. God would have to teach Moses a better way. In Luke, when Jesus was about to raise Lazarus from the dead, Martha basically says, "What are You doing? He's been dead four days, and he's gonna stink!" Want a miracle, even if it smells bad?

The words of men are powerful, aren't they? They can strip you of your "knowing" and cause you to settle for an easier path. While it's true that words can hurt you and cause you pain, it's still important to remember that they are just words. If you tell me I'm wonderful, it doesn't make me wonderful. In fact, just because you say it doesn't even mean you really believe it. If you tell me I'm horrible, your words don't make me that, either—even if you do believe it! Some words carry truth, and those are the words we should listen to. But when lies are shouted at us, when gossip from hell emerges, then they are just words, and we need to either ignore them or walk away, holding onto our victory.

When we believe a lie, we cannot come into agreement with the Lord and His intentions toward us. When we believe a lie, we disagree with God and the favor of God eludes us. When we believe a lie, we abandon the power of God in our lives.

David experienced this "War of the Words" when he was young, just before he killed Goliath. But he didn't listen to them. As he went to the camp of the Philistines to bring some corn, bread and cheese to his brothers who were fighting in the battle, this is the welcome that he received from his oldest brother, Eliab:

….Why camest thou down hither? And with whom hast thou left those few sheep in the wilderness? I know thy pride, and the naughtiness of thine heart; for thou art come down that thou mightest see the battle. And David said, What have I done now? Is there not a cause? (1 Samuel 17:28–29)

Can you believe it? Here was this little kid going to help. He brought gifts of food and was excited about the battle. Scripture tells us he got upset because he saw that the people were "dismayed and greatly afraid," and it made his insecure brother angry! David spoke up for the honor of God, and people hated him for it. He spoke up for the right cause, and they called him names because he made them look bad. His oldest brother said to him in anger, "What are you even doing here? You are full of pride and just want to see the battle. You are nothing but a loser, a sheepherder from the wilderness, and your flock is small and doesn't amount to anything, either. Why don't you just get lost?" David had to have endured this treatment more than once, because he says in verse 29, "What have I now done?" In other words, what's the problem now?

The Word goes on to say that David turned away from Eliab and starting giving his motivational speech to the other people, telling them that Goliath was nobody and that they were God's army, so they should fight. He told them that he would fight Goliath himself if the giant didn't quit bad-mouthing God. He took note that everyone was afraid and told them not to worry, that he would take Goliath out! King Saul even came along and told David, "Thou art not able to go against this Philistine to fight with him: for thou art but a youth, and he a man of war from his youth" (Exodus 2:33). But David wasn't falling for this trick of the enemy dressed up as a lie. In response, he quickly began to recite the greatness of the God he served. He turned from the negative people and all their gossip, and simply killed Goliath!

Let us gain our identity in Christ and Him alone, not the words of people. What would happen if we needed approval and confirmation so badly all the time that we became emotionally and spiritually handicapped without it? We would stop hearing the Lord and lean only on the words of men. What if the words were bad or provoked by evil? We set ourselves up, sometimes, when we have to hear words! Affirmation, confirmation, validation, recognition—all dangerous words that put an evil twist on the godly form of encouragement. Be careful of what you need!

Take a look at this story I heard one time:

> A group of frogs gathered together in their village to see who would win the mountain-climbing contest. Frogs came from near and far to compete. The mountain was tall, and rain was pouring down with great force.
>
> As most people know, frogs can be very negative creatures. The spectator frogs kept yelling from the base of the mountain to the competing frogs, "You'll never make it; you should come down now before you get hurt. It's getting dark. Aren't you getting tired and hungry? You are going to be so sore tomorrow you won't be able to go to work; come down, it's a dumb contest anyway...."
>
> One by one, the frogs began to drop off the mountainside, dejected and depressed. In the end, one frog made it to the top. All the naysayers began to cheer for joy and shout, for they had found their hero! The mayor frog spoke to the winning frog's mother, who was at the base of the mountain, and asked her why her son succeeded where others had failed. She smiled in her froggish way and said, "Because he is deaf!"

The minute you agree with people in order to please them, they will change their mind. The minute you decide not to pursue what God has told you to do in order to make others happy, they will despise you for not having any bravery. So you might as well save yourself some grief and go with God when He starts asking for you.

All those decisions that you made because somebody wanted you to, or you felt guilty if you didn't, or you were trapped by circumstances—give them to God. Because the Word says that what the enemy means for bad, that God will turn for good. We can trust Him with that. He will make a way to turn those bad decisions around when we yield to Him, even in the middle of our mistakes. Then, stop behaving like you are a victim of someone else's intentions. Be victorious in God's intentions and say "No!" when you need to, and run to "Yes!" only when God says to.

Life just got a whole lot simpler for you, now, didn't it?

CHAPTER 6

Looking and Turning

Moses was content to dwell with [Jethro] and he gave Moses Zipporah his daughter and she bare him a son and he called his name Gershom: for be said, I have been a stranger in a strange land (Exodus 2:21–22).

M oses was trying to work it out in Midian. The worst thing happened when he became content. Being content sitting by a well and dwelling in a land that is not yours, a land you are not called to defend or possess, is a formula for disaster. "Moses was content." Moses, the man of God, became merely a man from Midian.

In Philippians 4:11, Paul said, "I have learned, in whatsoever state I am, therewith to be content." The word "content" in this instance, according to *Vine's Expository Dictionary*, means "self-sufficient, adequate, needing no assistance." But this is not the kind of "content" that Moses was talking about. When the Word says that "Moses was content," it is not saying that he was satisfied and feeling sufficient. These are two completely different words.

In the context of Exodus 2, the word "content" (*yaal*, #H2974) means "(…through the idea of mental weakness)…to yield, especially assent." The fact that Moses was content means that he was settling for what was second best for him, and he knew it. He was depressed and apathetic.

Moses was willing to be weak. This is an ailment he had suffered since he stepped foot in Midian to search for God. When we allow our minds to become weak and give in to yielding decisions and foolishness, we will become depressed and feel alone just as Moses did.

> *Now Moses kept the flock of Jethro his father in law, the priest of Midian: and he led the flock to the backside of the desert and came to the mountain of God, even to Horeb. And the angel of the Lord appeared unto him in a flame of fire out of the midst of a bush: and he looked and, behold, the bush burned with fire, and the bush was not consumed. And Moses said, I will now turn aside and see this great sight, why the bush is not burnt. And when the Lord saw that he turned aside to see, God called unto him out of the midst of the bush and said, Moses, Moses. And he said, Here am I. And He said, Draw not nigh hither: put off thy shoes from off thy feet, for the place whereon thou standest is holy ground. Moreover He said, I am the God of thy father, the God of Abraham, the God of Isaac, and the God of Jacob. And Moses hid his face; for he was afraid to look upon God* (Exodus 3:1–6).

Forty years had passed since Moses fled from who he was with all his insecurities. Even after all this time, the flock was still not his. He was tending another man's goods and was content doing it. He was busy doing the wrong things, just killing time. Killing time and preparing are two different things. Killing time is mindless; preparing has purpose!

Until Moses fled the face of Pharaoh and let the prince of Egypt in him die, he was not ready to see the burning bush. It took 40 years for him to get ready because he was tending another man's goods, instead of inflicting the deathblow to self. It is easy to tend another man's goods when you are just trying to survive. It is easy to tend another man's goods when you are no longer sure of who you are. It is easy to tend another man's goods when you are worried about the words of someone else and walking with festering wounds. It's easy to tend another man's sheep when you don't want any responsibility.

When Jacob tended Laban's sheep, he eventually made them his own. When David tended sheep, he left them behind to lead a nation. Tending sheep is not bad if that is what you are supposed to do, but if God has another plan for you, you should not be content tending those sheep!

The Backside of the Mountain

Could it be that Moses was keeping the flock near the mountain of God to have a reason to go to the backside of the desert? He wanted to know who God was, but passion wasn't leading him. He wasn't sure what it meant to meet God and wasn't convinced of the journey or what it would require, so he stayed in the shadows, just in case. He kept going around the backside of the mountain that represented God, but he had never before faced it head on.

We can be involved with God and not really participate in His plan for us. We can be acquainted with Him but never have a conversation with Him. We can know His name but never allow our lives to be affected by Him. This is what the backside of God's mountain represents. We can only get away with this for so long before God comes calling—even if we're in our sacred sanctuary shrouded in fear, hiding on the backside of the mountain, hoping not to be discovered.

Moses was coming to the turning point of his life and finally decided to stop hiding from his destiny. He had to decide if fellowship with God was worth the trip beyond relationship. He was wounded and insecure and not sure of exactly who God was. But he made a move toward God, and God noticed it.

Relationship with God can cause us to call His name for a lifetime, never being changed by who He is. It will allow us to hide on the backside of the mountain. But fellowship will abide by the burning bush, causing us to crave the heart of God and make the decision to gain it at all costs. Fellowship goes past calling His name and lives where you know Him.

For example, I have never met Rev. Billy Graham, but I know his name. We have a relationship: he's a preacher, and I'm a listener. We don't have a fellowship within that relationship because I couldn't tell you for the life of me what his favorite food is; that would take having a fellowship with him.

The angel of the Lord appeared to Moses in a flame in the middle of a burning bush. He noticed that the bush was burning but wasn't being consumed. He stood for a moment, wondering about it. That's what he was doing at this point, nothing more—and God was watching.

Often, when the Lord is trying to get our attention, that's what we do. We notice something, look at it, wonder about it, and try to figure it out. We can be at this stage for 40 minutes or 40 years. We could spend an entire lifetime there, talking about it and never doing anything about it; seeing it, but never experiencing it.

The other day, as I walked by a group of people, someone called for me to come over. They'd been having a discussion about weight lifting, and this man wanted me to tell the group that he knew about lifting and that he had gone to school to learn about nutrition and fitness. He used to be an authority on the subject, and I suppose he felt he wasn't being respected. I said I didn't know what he knew about weight lifting. I knew that he used to lift weights, but I really didn't know what he knew or what he was doing now. He begged me to tell them how knowledgeable he was on this subject. So I took him aside and said, "Listen, you are a tall, skinny guy with basically no muscles. If you want people to believe that you know how to get muscles, you ought to have a few. You are like a fat man trying to sell a diet, or a bald man telling people how to grow hair."

A Trust Issue

One day long ago, Moses believed he was supposed to do something through God. But it was God who would do something through him. God had chosen him, but would he agree? He knew what God's plan for him was. He knew what was on God's mind. Was he embarrassed? Was he afraid of failing again? Could he ever trust this God who appeared to have let him down and hung him out to dry, as an Egyptian lay dead at his feet? It's hard to say if Moses had these thoughts, or if he truly understood that he had gotten ahead of God, and his motives had been wrong. Wounded faith will cause you to gain identity from a failed prayer or hope. *Moses was wounded, and he had to find the courage to believe again.*

We do the same thing to God when we have entrusted something to Him and it goes badly. We entrust our marriage, children, job, safety and sanity to Him. Then, when something apparently goes wrong, we decide that, although we still love the Lord, we shall not trust Him anymore. It's a painful experience that we bury quickly in our hearts, and the wounds can fester there for years, often never being discovered. *A lack of trust will prevent faith from growing.*

Perhaps Moses blamed God for his whole mess. Was his mistake really God's fault? Or would he come to a place where he would understand that killing someone and then running away had little to do with God? Would he ever discover that truth and trust again? Oh, the ponderings of Moses at that moment!

When you are window-shopping, you usually stay outside for quite a while, where no one will bother you. And usually, you have no real intention of buying. But there are those times when something compels you to enter the store. Experienced window-shoppers will watch until the very last possible moment before they give up their spot on the sidewalk and enter into the domain of those who are paying a price. The Word says to count the cost before taking action, and Moses was doing that.

We only have to trust God enough to let Him overcome the fears that hold us back.

While Moses was looking, God was not compelled to respond. I'm sure He was there and watching, but He doesn't do much with people who are just looking. He loves them, but He does not count on them. Lookers usually move on. We do that with callings and duties we are afraid of and feel incapable of accomplishing. When we are looking and nothing more, we have forgotten that the Lord said that He is our strength in our weakness.

We don't have to do anything based on our ability; God will do it based on His own ability. We only have to trust God enough to let

Him overcome the fears that hold us back. The rumbling bush roars at us: "You are not rejected; you are accepted. You can trust Me."

Then it happened. Moses took action.

> *Moses said, I will now turn aside and see this great sight, why the bush is not burnt. And when the Lord saw that he turned aside, God called unto him out of the midst of the bush and said, Moses, Moses. And he said, Here am I* (Exodus 3:3–4).

Notice how the Lord doesn't respond openly until Moses moves past looking and starts turning. "He turns aside to see…."

The Word doesn't say that when the Lord saw Moses looking, He spoke to him. Lots of people look. Lots of people will see someone go through something and tell the story, but it is not their story. They may have your story, or their grandfather's story or their mother's story, but they don't have their own story because they would have to do more than just look to get a story like the one Moses was going to get.

Maybe you are looking right now. It's easy to look and talk about how great it would be. It's easy to sit down by the well and talk about it. It's easy to tend another man's sheep and not assume any of the liability or real responsibility. It's easy to walk around the backside of the mountain and talk about what you saw from far away, void of any current experience.

When you are climbing up the side of the mountain and have stopped midway, altered your path and turned toward the flame, that is when you know you shall never use your lawn chair down by the well again. At that moment, you are unsure of where you are going, but very sure of who is going with you.

When we "turn aside to see," the Lord is immediately there with redemption and restoration. It's amazing to see how quickly He puts His glory upon us. The Lord saw Moses turn aside to look, and then God called his name out of the fire. It was another critical moment of decision for Moses: Would he stay or flee again? God was just waiting for Moses to be more interested in what God was doing than in the contentment he had found with the flock in the desert. Moses hadn't agreed with God about anything yet, but he was willing to listen.

Moses was told about the holy ground. When Moses was merely looking, he certainly didn't understand that it was actually holy ground that he was standing upon. Mere lookers don't know about that—only those who behave as chosen people do. Those are people who are willing to walk with Him and invest in their relationship to gain fellowship. When Moses stopped what he was doing and lent his ear to God, when he turned aside from his own agenda, then he came to know that he was standing on holy ground.

He had a haunting question earlier: "Why isn't the bush burnt?" The Lord said to him in Exodus 3:5, "Draw not nigh hither; put off thy shoes from off thy feet, for the place whereon thou standest is holy ground." The burning bush was not consumed because miracles abound on holy ground. God proceeded to remind Moses of who He was, and Moses was "afraid to look upon God" (verse 6).

God's Plan

God called to Moses, "Come a little closer, just a little closer. I want to see you close up and I want to show you My great love for you. Come up to this holy ground. You won't need your shoes up here; you won't need anything, for I AM here. Come to Me just as you are, for I AM enough. There is a miracle up here waiting for you as a token of My affection for you; won't you come and see it? Won't you come and warm your weary soul next to its flame?"

God Himself proceeded to tell Moses His plan.

> *I am come down to deliver them out of the hand of the Egyptians, and to bring them up out of that land unto a good land... flowing with milk and honey....Come now therefore, and I will send thee unto Pharaoh that thou mayest bring forth my people the children of Israel out of Egypt (Exodus 3:7–10).*

In response, Moses began to tell God about his unworthiness: "Who am I, that I should go unto Pharaoh" (verse 11). God told Moses not to worry about it—that He would be with him—but Moses wasn't buying it. He told God that he didn't really know God well enough to represent Him. Moses started to get to the root of his problem when he said, "When I tell the people that God sent me, the people will say to me, 'What is His name?'" With Moses, it was the people, the people and their words. It had been 40 years, and still people's opinions and words mattered more to him than God's.

The last words spoken to him in Egypt were the first ones he remembered when God came calling. The thought of going back to Egypt for any reason, when the memory of its cruelty was still shouting at him, made it hard to start the journey. The painful, untruthful words of others had lingered in his mind over the last four decades, and now they would emerge with a haunting rendition of negative reinforcement. I'm sure those words were rarely silent and especially now, as God is calling him forward, the words call him backward as they pound in his chest and confuse his mind, "Who made you a judge and ruler over us?" Moses was a man who had been captured by the words of others, and now he would have to begin to trust the God he was attempting to serve in order to be set free from the rejection of them.

God was doing a lot of talking to Moses. Throughout Exodus 3 and 4, God showed some of the greatest examples of long-suffering patience that you will find anywhere in the Bible. God told Moses that He was coming to deliver the people and that He was going to be moving through Moses to do it. Remember what we read earlier? Moses knew all along that this was God's plan. It had been 40 years, and the plan still hadn't changed.

The rejection and depression that Moses was still suffering from were tempting him to flee. He was still responding to the deep wounds in his heart, rather than to the holy power that he was facing.

At this point, Moses was Batman without the cool car, Superman without the cape, Samson with no hair, Noah without an ark, David without a slingshot. It's tough when you know you are supposed to do something and don't have the goods to get it done! The lesson Moses needed to learn as he descended the mountain into Egypt was this: how to trust God so he would be able to lean on Him.

I guess we need to ask ourselves why we stand on the backside of the mountain in the middle of the desert and miss so many opportunities to live in abundant truth that only climbing the mountain can give.

When the Lord calls us to "come up" to where He is, He will enable every step we take toward Him. Can't you see the bush burning and don't you hear Him calling your name ever so gently? He says, "Give those wounds to Me so I can bring healing to your broken heart and hurting soul. I know they hurt you, but you can trust Me!"

He longs to show you who He is—He's not the God who hides on the backside of anything. You can't fully know Him there. He will love you there, but you can't fully know Him until you come out from hiding behind that mountain of yourself. You can trust Him. He will bring you out and lift you up.

This is the same God who, with all the drama of heaven, proclaimed loudly from a burning bush on a sacred mountain, "I Am God!" And He is the same God who whispers in your ear as He places His hand upon your heart, "I love you and I won't hurt you. You can trust Me—come a little closer!" Can't you hear Him sing the song to you, "Softly and tenderly, Jesus is calling, come home, come home…"?

CHAPTER 7

Causes of Rejection

Moses is stuck in Midian because of the spirit of rejection. He has chosen a quiet, little, comfortable life that he can have complete control over because he has lost his identity to his wounds and is paralyzed at the thought of moving on. As Moses heads back to Egypt to collect his brethren, the Lord would go to great lengths to prove to him that he was accepted, not rejected.

> *To the praise of the glory of his grace, wherein he hath made us accepted in the beloved* (Ephesians 1:6)

The *Merriam-Webster Dictionary* tells us that to "reject" is "to refuse to accept, consider...to refuse to hear, receive or admit... throw back, repulse."

Rejection comes upon people innocently enough most of the time. For instance, I was on an airplane flying back from Central America and was sitting next to a woman who had a toddler. He was an active boy and wasn't happy to be on a long airplane flight. Mom was doing the best she could, but then she became angry. Many of us have been there.

There was another boy sitting directly across the aisle from us who had a different temperament. He seemed to enjoy the ride and was easily amused. (I was wishing I had been seated next to that kid!)

Anyway, then it happened. Rejection came flying out of the depths of hell and landed on this anxious little boy next to me. The mother shouted at him, "Why can't you be good like that other little boy? See how good he is being for his mother? Why can't you be good like that?" Deed done!

My heart screamed at the horror of what the mother had done to that boy. The knowledge that she would inevitably reinforce this message repeatedly throughout his life became a constant pain to me during that flight. Did she mean to do that? No. Do any of us mean to do that? No. But does it still happen? Yes, it does! Many of us don't find out until decades later that when we were being formed in our early years, rejection became one of the pieces of our puzzle.

The spirit of rejection will cause us to gravitate toward the common and comfortable thing in an attempt to never suffer rejection again. At the same time, it is desperate to find situations where we are rejected, so it can be validated. Rejection is an insidious, two-sided coin that never quits flipping until you are delivered from it.

Rejection brings, among other things, a fear of failure that provokes us to make mistakes. Whether it be subconsciously or overtly, we usually try very hard to be accepted by people, and it's one of the biggest mistakes we can make in life.

They say that rejection is the number one cause of suicide, especially among school-age children and young adults. It is also said that on the average, 75 percent of what we hear and think is negative. Many of us have been conditioned or predisposed to thinking negative things because we have heard them for so long. Once we believe that we are rejected, we begin not only to behave as rejected people, but we quietly, in the privacy of our own mind, reinforce those thoughts to ourselves.

Enlightening Survey

I have taken my own little, somewhat unscientific, but nonetheless enlightening survey this year. I interviewed more than 500 people. These people were all ages and came from various parts of the country, representing different nationalities, ethnicities, cultures and religious denominations. There were athletes, artists, professionals, celebrities, factory workers, office workers and volunteers. Some were in ministry, and others did not even know Christ at the time of the interview. The purpose of my survey was to find out which human emotion would evoke the most fear in someone and ultimately prevent them from fully pursuing the purpose of their lives.

After a 40-day water fast and much prayer, the Lord presented me with five emotional objects of fear, and I developed my survey from them. I told the people nothing about the survey or its purpose, but just asked them a straight question: "Which of these emotions brings a fear upon you that would possibly, above all other things, prevent you from doing something you felt that you should?"

1. Insecurity (I'm not sure of my ability.)
2. Abuse (I don't want to be hurt.)
3. Instability (I'm not sure of the situation I am entering into.)
4. Rejection (The people or situation will not accept me.)
5. Failure (I will be unsuccessful in my venture.)

Out of the 507 people surveyed, a remarkable 412 said that rejection was their greatest fear. Failure and insecurity tied for second place, and most of those people said they were afraid of failure because that would make them feel rejected. Many who cited insecurity as their number one cause offered this information: they were insecure about their abilities because they had been rejected in the past. That statement seems to be the slogan for the "Acceptable Affliction of Mankind" fan club! Remember, these people had no idea I was pondering the state of rejection upon mankind. It's epidemic!

When we are young and vulnerable to rejection, it sets the pace and program for our whole life. We will either overcome and be stronger because of it or spend a lifetime trying to deal with it, never feeling quite good enough. Note that most of the reasons people gave me for feeling rejected stemmed from their childhood. Childhood is an innocent time in that sometimes, you get what you didn't earn and didn't ask for. God help us to recover from emotionally devouring our young.

Since it seemed that we had an epidemic on our hands, I thought it was important to know more about the people who were in my survey. It appeared that many of these people had been formed by the "Moses Method of Rejection." I started to ask questions as part of the survey to find out why they were so afraid and insecure. Here's a summary of some of their stories.

When they were young, they remember that their parents never picked them up on time. Their parents rarely, if ever, attended any of their academic or sporting events. Many said that they were products of divorce (in fact, most of them were). That made sense. They said there was a time in life when they had to be in control because nobody else was. Many said that when they were young, they felt their parents chose other people and other things above them. As adults, they had experienced all kinds of unfaithful relationships and were often victims of adultery. Many were the children of missionaries and pastors and felt that their parents chose ministry above them.

One man cried as he told me that his mother was on the phone for as long as he could remember, and it always made him mad. He would always act up while she was on the phone to get her attention. I think his anger was his way of desperately trying to prevent his mother from being on the phone, so that he could prevent that bitter seed from lodging in his soul. I think he knew that it was a bad thing and deep inside was desperate to prevent it from happening. He said his mother used to just yell at him to be quiet. He felt like someone who was drowning and screaming for help. In his words, "I know it's dumb, but I couldn't help feeling like she didn't want me around, even though I know that's not true. But I still struggle with that in relationships today. And to this day, I can't stand it when someone is on the phone while I'm there, visiting them."

Such a shame that we are not taught at an early age how to "read" the road signs of human behavior. The boy didn't want to be emotionally abused and the mother probably never dreamed that she was putting that on her son. Yet for all the good intentions in the world, there it is.

Another childhood situation that was often recalled was teasing from bullies on the playground (although a lot of that is unavoidable, when a child is never healed by love and acceptance at home, the devil gets a free ride).

Then there were those things connected to adult life and spiritual things: failures in business, marriage, education, employment and life in general. People wept as they talked about their disappointments with the people around them, with their children or with the Lord. Most of the pain didn't happen today; it was pain that had wrinkles and was well-aged.

Some people misunderstood the elements of healing and so they prayed "wrong," and it appeared to them that their prayers fell to the ground. People died, decisions that were made thinking God was in it destroyed them, leaving them hopeless and spiritually broke. So they came to a place where they didn't want to trust the Lord anymore; they felt rejected and abandoned by God, simply because they didn't understand the same things God did. Were they rejected? No! Did they feel that way and was that perceived rejection painful? Yes!

No matter what your occupation, you are meant to live in the joy of the Lord.

All those things that have developed around you, even as a child, to form your reasoning and heart must be evaluated. Do they edify the Lord and others, or are they symptoms of a root of rejection in your life, spilling onto those around you? Here's a question that may help you: "Is there always a conflict or problem in my life?" No matter what your occupation, you are meant to live in the joy of the Lord. When you are continually in conflict, you have to ask yourself if maybe, just maybe, you are the cause and creator of that conflict. Remember, rejection wants to maintain its position in your heart and residency in your soul, so it will find many ways to be reinforced by causing you to feel rejected. It will actually create scenarios by which it can shout its control over you. Is that happening to you?

Jesus overcame your spirit of rejection when you asked Him to; but now you must deal with the rest of you, with His help. Your body, soul and mind must learn how to agree with the Spirit of God in you. When you are delivered, your responsibility is to behave that way. The devil is a liar, and nothing will ever change that.

CHAPTER 8

Effects of Rejection

As we follow the life of Moses, a few things are abundantly clear. One of them is that he was a man who walked out the cure for his rejection. Moses went from being a man to being a vessel because, in the midst of his own identity crisis and spiritual inability, he was able to keep showing up. Watch Moses and, perhaps, you will see yourself as he struggled to reconcile his wounds with his faith.

Years ago, I was speaking at a conference, and I knew that God wanted to set some people free from unforgiveness. I asked how many of them wanted to forgive and had tried doing so in the past, but the problem kept coming back to captivate them. I also asked if there were some who just couldn't quite get over their anger. Although they had tried and felt that they had forgiven the person, the situation still bugged them, and the rage wouldn't leave. I then asked them to stand if this described them. The tragedy was that about two-thirds of these people stood. There were both joy and tears. I know they were excited because they felt I knew what to do, but I didn't. I prayed for them but did not sense a release in the spirit.

Clearly, the Lord had revealed this to me, so I asked Him if He'd now go ahead and provide me with a cure. I had never seen this tragedy in mass form before, and the answer that God gave me was a revelation. The Lord told me that rejection is what was holding these people in the bondage of unforgiveness. So, we went to prayer, and Jesus destroyed that root of rejection and then they were able to forgive. Unforgiveness was a symptom of rejection. The people were set free!

Rejection will cause symptoms to be planted in our lives. These symptoms are safely hidden within that root of rejection, which often goes undetected for years. Deliverance becomes complicated and ineffectual when the stronghold root is not addressed.

Our True Identity

We must find our identity in Christ alone, not in another person or their words, not in a ministry or a job, not in a family or cause. He has not rejected us, but accepted us. He has not forsaken us, but embraced us. Second Corinthians 4:6–10 declares,

> *For God who commanded the light to shine out of darkness, hath shined in our hearts, to give the light of the knowledge of the glory of God in the face of Jesus Christ. But we have this treasure in earthen vessels, that the excellency of the power may be of God and not of us. We are troubled on every side, yet not distressed; we are perplexed, but not in despair; persecuted, but not forsaken; cast down, but not destroyed.*

All this care and concern over us comes because the face of Christ is steadfastly gazing upon us, never flinching.

By-products or fruits of the spirit of rejection become rampant in our lives when we have held onto the wounds from rejection and abandonment. What are these branches on the tree of rejection that grow from the root of pain within us? I have compiled a list of main offenders. This list is not exclusive, but it deals with the majority of emotional ailments that I have observed as the Holy Spirit has pointed them out. You are unique and wonderfully made; ask the Lord if some of these apply to you, or if you have other symptoms that gain their identity from the root of rejection. He will guide you in all truth.

Following are seven of the symptoms that your life will shout if you have been stung by rejection:

1. Lack of trust (Disappointments produce dislike of change and feelings of unworthiness.)
2. Pride (It justifies your correction of others and refuses correction for yourself.)
3. Fear (especially of failure)
4. Need for control (You are anxious and worried until you get it.)
5. Jealousy (It causes you to find fault with others and to envy.)
6. Insecurity (You feel guilt and shame, which at times can make you willing to cause another to look bad in an attempt to make yourself look good.)
7. Unforgiveness (It is often created by bitterness, which is usually married to hatred. Together, they wage war on anything that will try to prevent rejection. Unforgiveness of others often comes because we cannot forgive ourselves. When rejection is part of our unforgiveness toward others, the enemy reminds us of our past failures to torment us and create more guilt and rejection.)

When these things have been wrapped tightly around our souls, we will often pretend to walk in their cure; but we never allow ourselves to fully embrace the cure or be changed by the truth it represents.

If you've been rejected, you will find yourself defending your right not to change, almost at all costs. You will tell yourself you are okay, but when the relationships around you fall apart, you will keep making excuses as to why it's okay. You will argue to defend positions that probably have no real bearing on your life, and you always have a need to be "right." Rejection doesn't want to get "found out," so it wears these seven coats as a covering, hoping to never be discovered. *As rejection controls you, it will cause you to be controlling of the people and situations around you.*

A need for control indicates a lack of trust.
A lack of trust will create a weak faith.

A need for control indicates a lack of trust. A lack of trust will create a weak faith. Weak faith produces fear, and when you have fear, you have imperfect love. According to 1 John 4 and Galatians 5, "Perfect love casts out fear and love makes faith operate." The Word also says that "without faith it is impossible to please (agree with) God." Further, "Faith comes by hearing and hearing by the Word of God."

It appears that love would be at the bottom of this mess trying to rise up and speak. Her words are the ones that will destroy fear and produce faith.

Acceptance and Rejection

When we have a spirit of rejection, we have a glaring need to be both accepted and rejected at the same time. A rejected person will often bring opportunities to be further rejected upon themselves. For instance, suppose Sally, Sue and Sarah came to visit Jane. Jane says to Sally, "Those are great shoes!" Sarah says, "Yeah, those really are!" Sue says, "What about MY shoes?" Jane says, "That's a great haircut, Sarah!" Sally says, "Yeah, who cut your hair?" Sue says, "What about MY hair?" Jane says, "You look like you lost weight, Sue." Sue says, "So, you're saying that I was fat before?" Sue desperately wants to be loved and accepted, but at the same time, she must reinforce and validate the core of rejection in her being. So she will find reasons or create reasons to be rejected. Often, to accommodate this incessant need to be rejected, someone carrying the spirit of rejection within themselves has the strongholds of self-hatred and self-rejection. This is when we begin to feel like we aren't quite good enough, and we will never measure up. Often, many of these people are driven in an effort to overcome the root that continually shouts defeat at them.

Samuel was a child who was dropped off at Mount Shiloh after he was weaned to be raised by Eli the priest, an incapable father. Let us now visit Samuel for a moment as a man. According to 1 Samuel 8, Samuel felt rejected when the people demanded a king in his place. Basically, the people "fired" him. Samuel was the judge at the time and caretaker of the people, so this broke his heart. The Lord came and told Samuel, "The people haven't rejected you; they have rejected Me."

In fact, the word "displeased" that is used in this sentence, "the thing displeased Samuel, when they said, Give us a king to judge us" (1 Samuel 8:6), means that he was really mad! When Samuel was given up as a child after he was weaned in 1 Samuel 1:24, he was about the same age that Moses was when he was taken to Pharaoh's doorstep many years earlier. Was it wrong that Samuel was given to the Lord's work like he was? No, but perhaps it was mishandled. It is recorded that his parents visited him only once a year.

"The people have not rejected YOU, but they have rejected ME!" If he wasn't feeling the sting of rejection, he would not have needed this reminder. With God's reality check, Samuel recovered quickly. The thing I love about Samuel is that he heard God when He spoke and was willing to let go of what was trying to hold him hostage to pain.

When we have rejection or an unhealed wound in our past, we often take injustices around us very personally and always find ourselves in some kind of trauma.

In 1 Kings 19, why did Elijah find that cave? Even though God had accepted him, the people rejected him and it brought depression. Depression is a horrible gift that can be given to us by the spirit of rejection.

If the enemy can get us to believe we are rejected and not accepted, he has won ground. But the Holy Spirit is able to destroy those roots of rejection in an instant. He is hovering and moving above your head right now. All He needs is for you to agree with God, and He will get busy performing the perfection of all good things in your life.

To determine if the spirit of rejection is alive in us, we have to be honest enough to ask if we have these symptoms manifesting in our lives. If you are unsure, ask a trusted friend or your spouse if you are afflicted with this emotional ailment. Ask your parents or your pastor. Perhaps they can see what you cannot. Perhaps they will speak words that you have not been willing to hear until now. Sometimes when we get so busy protecting our pain, we can't hear the Lord anymore.

Unless Moses was willing to step aside and let the Lord take his rejection and his wounds away, he would not have been able to endure the sands of Egypt as they led him back to the people who rejected him. No matter what your gifts, if you are not willing to stop being the walking wounded, you will only walk in circles because your gifts will not be trusted, even though your heart is good and your God is great. The walking wounded minister out of their pain, and in the process, can destroy their gifts and everyone around them!

The Cure
So, how do we get released from this spirit of rejection? Here are some simple steps for you to follow as you give your willingness to be moved by the Holy Spirit up to God today. He is able if you are willing.

1. "Confess your faults one to another…that ye may be healed" (James 5:16).

    Confess! Admit your wounds and errors. Confession takes the power away from the enemy and leads to repentance.
2. "The Lord is not slack concerning his promise, as some men count slackness; but is longsuffering to us-ward, not willing that any should perish, but that all should come to repentance" (2 Peter 3:9).

    Repent! Repentance breaks the barriers of rejection.
3. "For he hath made him to be sin for us, who knew no sin; that we might be made the righteousness of God in him" (2 Corinthians 5:21).

    Be free! Knowing that you no longer carry your sin brings freedom.
4. "Stand fast therefore in the liberty wherewith Christ hath made us free, and be not entangled again with the yoke of bondage" (Galatians 5:1).

    Sin no more! Freedom from bondage in the heart and mind bring liberty in the spirit. You must believe you are free and not entertain actions and attitudes of rejection any longer. Jesus Christ came so that you could be free. Make it count and know that He has made you worthy and righteous before God!

5. "As it is written, For thy sake we are killed all the day long; we are accounted as sheep for the slaughter. Nay, in all these things we are more than conquerors through him that loved us. For I am persuaded, that neither death, nor life, nor angels, nor principalities, nor powers, nor things present, nor things to come, nor height, nor depth, nor any other creature, shall be able to separate us from the love of God, which is in Christ Jesus our Lord" (Romans 8:36–42).

Know that you are loved! You are accepted, adored and cherished by your Lord and Savior Jesus Christ and the Father who sent Him. You have a heavenly inheritance of power and overcoming ability in Him. He will never leave you or forsake you. Your Father in heaven looks upon you with everlasting loving-kindness. He loves you with supernatural affection and has sent the angels to go before you to prepare the way that you should go.

Let Jesus be your strength in this moment and choose to be made new. You will have to make daily choices to not behave in a rejected way anymore. Your body, soul, spirit and mind have to all agree, and sometimes that takes some training. God will redefine the way you do things and protect you like you have never known. Just trust Him.

CHAPTER 9

But…But…But

And Moses said unto God, Who am I, that I should go unto Pharaoh, and that I should bring forth the children of Israel out of Egypt? And he said, Certainly I will be with thee; and this shall be a token unto thee, that I have sent thee: When thou hast brought forth the people out of Egypt, ye shall serve God upon this mountain. And Moses said unto God, Behold, when I come unto the children of Israel, and shall say unto them, The God of your fathers hath sent me unto you; and they shall say to me, What is his name? What shall I say unto them? And God said unto Moses, I AM THAT I AM: and He said, Thus shalt thou say unto the children of Israel, I AM hath sent me unto you (Exodus 3:11–14).

God told Moses to tell the people that His name is "I AM THAT I AM…thus shalt thou say unto the children of Israel, I AM hath sent me unto you." God continued to instruct and encourage Moses, letting him know that He would be with him every step of the way. He spent time reminding Moses who He really was and letting him know that he would never be alone. But, unfortunately, the negative words that someone had spoken to Moses 40 years earlier had had time to fester. He was convinced that he would be unable to follow God's plan and was bound to the failure of his past. Remember, the guy was talking to a burning bush this entire time!

The Lord gave Moses information concerning the journey to comfort him. God said that Moses would return to the mountain and worship Him with all the people after he brought them out of Egypt. What a beautiful picture for his heart to carry as he went forward on a very intimidating task! God's plan was to bring the Israelites back through Midian, the stomping ground of Moses. He would come full circle back to this "talking mountain," Mount Horeb, the mountain of God, also known as Mount Zion. Moses had been living in this land for 40 years, and I'm sure that he knew it very well. It was no longer a strange land that God was taking them through to get to Canaan; it was the land of Moses, the man from Midian. God gave great consideration to Moses in the mapping of the journey, just as He gives us the same consideration, even though it may not appear that way at times.

The Lord told Moses that He knew all about the horrible affliction of the people (a cause that Moses killed for earlier), and that He wanted to deliver them out of it and into a wonderful promised land. The Lord hardly ever just simply delivers us out of trouble, for He loves to deliver us out of trouble and into abundance. This is what He was doing for Moses. He continually said, "I'm going to deliver them because I love them and have heard their cry. Then I'm going to bring you to a prosperous and abundant place that someone else owns right now; but we are going to remove them, and I'm going to give you the best land that there is. I'm going to kill the giants. The most you'll have to do is step over them as they fall!"

God was honest with Moses and let him know that, after Moses asked the Pharaoh to let the people go, Pharaoh would not agree to do it. God told Moses that He would then stretch out His mighty hand and "smite Egypt with all my wonders which I will do in the midst thereof: and after that he will let you go. I will give this people favour in the sight of the Egyptians: and it shall come to pass, that, when ye go, ye shall not go empty" (Exodus 3:20–21). God told them they were going to take the jewelry, gold and fine clothing from the Egyptians when they left. God gives great and mighty promises here. He was saying, "Just agree with Me and all this favor will fall upon you." But Moses continued his argument with God.

Moses answered God, "...But, behold, they will not believe me, nor hearken unto my voice: for they will say, the Lord hath not appeared unto thee" (Exodus 4:1). It seems like we have heard this before. It's a different flavor, but the same dish. The man is in a panic.

I remember, when I was in my teenage years, the Lord asked me to do a very hard thing. I began to exhaust my argument with God using these two sentences of dispute, which were birthed out of a fear of rejection. My vocabulary was forever changed. I said, "But Lord..." and "What if..." God told me, "The 'But Lords' and the 'What ifs' of this world will make your heart too small for My plan. 'But Lord' and 'What if' come from people without a purpose, and I've given you one." The Lord continued, "Your job is to obey and My job is to perform the purpose of that obedience." Needless to say, I have never again said "But Lord" or "What if." Pointless excuses can cause us to disagree with God and miss His favor. When people agree with God, it produces divine influence upon them and through them.

When we begin to let the external things dictate our faith, then the internal things begin to shake and rattle, and all of a sudden, it's as if we never believed at all. We begin to doubt and question. *Then the voice in our head and the fear in our heart seem to marry one another and create a force stronger than our will.*

Moses knew who he was, but 40 years in the desert, playing with his calling and purpose, caused him to doubt his destiny and wonder what he was truly created to do. Moses was experiencing times of questioning and doubting in the desert. But we must, at all costs, never allow the doubt to overcome us, or we shall never walk back to Egypt and take the land.

I'm sure his negative self-talk was on the high scale for the national negative survey. Are you so worried about being wrong that you never risk being right? This was the affliction of Moses!

The Lord is long-suffering. After Moses came up with another excuse to not obey, God spoke to him and showed Moses His power and protection. What we see in Exodus 4 is an amazing effort made by God, the Almighty Creator of the universe, reaching out to His creation—a man who is consumed with insecurities that are seeking to destroy his favor.

The rod of Moses turned into a snake, and Moses pulled back. The Lord told Moses to grab it by the tail, and he did. The snake returned to the form of a rod. The Lord turned one of Moses's hands leprous. A moment later, He healed it. God told Moses, "I have appeared to you and they will know it. They will believe you, and I will back you up. If you are still worried about them not believing you, then know this, as you pour water on the ground in front of them, I will turn it into blood." Moses ran out of ways to say, "They won't believe me!" The Lord took away all his excuses by showing Moses who He was. If you have been unforgiving in the past and have been set free from it, your mind can still tend to default to that position and wander there out of habit. If you have been a victim, you must be careful not to behave that way any longer, once you've been set free. Once you learn how to judge and gossip, it is difficult to unlearn that, but you must. Once you have been set free from addiction, you have to resist the temptation your body could bring upon you to engage in that activity again. If the devil is no longer holding you to it, then you would be foolish to hold yourself there. Often, sick people adopt sick tendencies simply because they are comfortable there and are used to being "the sick one." But the cell door is open—we just need to walk out.

We must bring our bodies under subjection to Jesus Christ and gain our identity in Him alone—not from unforgiveness, sickness, poverty, abuse or any of the other things this world would love to put on us.

Remember, if you have been rejected and carry that spirit with you, you will actually find reasons (many of which are fabricated) to feed your need to be rejected. Many horrors are not real after deliverance, but imagined. Jeremiah 9:14 says, "[They] have walked after the imagination of their own heart, and after [the devil], which their fathers taught them."

It would appear that the only thing left for Moses to do was agree with God. To say, "Okay, maybe they will believe me, and if they don't, You'll set them straight, anyway. So what do I have to lose? I will obey." That would have been the desired response. But instead we hear him mumbling, "Oh, but wait, there is this other thing I can shout to God about, instead of obeying Him..."

The Next Delusion
Moses quickly embarked on his next journey of delusion. And the amazing thing is, he did it right in front of God; the One who just set a snake loose in front of him and then made it turn into a stick, the One who caused his hand to be leprous and then recover. God said, "I have the power to lift up or cast down. I am in charge and I can fix any mess that you have." But somewhere, Moses found the stupidity (or courage—I don't know which one it was) to say to the God of all, whom he had been conversing with and interacting with as the flame in a burning bush, "O my Lord, I am not eloquent, neither heretofore, nor since thou hast spoken unto thy servant; but I am slow of speech and of a slow tongue" (Exodus 4:10). The problem is, Moses isn't talking to his neighbor—he is talking to God, and God knows everything.

Acts 7:22 has Stephen, in his famous speech of defense before the Jewish High Priest and Council, making this observation: "And Moses was learned in all the wisdom of the Egyptians and was mighty in words and in deeds." Please remember, we are at the burning bush back in Exodus. There is a constant and continual reminder in front of Moses, beyond the snake and the leprosy and the powerful voice being spoken by a flame, there is this bush that won't be consumed by the fire.

Earlier in his life, Moses was a keynote speaker. He knew the language and was eloquently trained to rule. For a man who was raised as the prince of Egypt, who history tells us "was learned in all the wisdom of the Egyptians and was mighty in words and in deeds," he was acting very strangely. His insecurities seem to jump out and grab me at this point in the story. When he says that he is not an eloquent speaker and he is slow of speech and tongue, what he is saying is that's the way he is now. He was not always that way, but he is now! He developed his handicaps through his wounds. Isn't he describing a man who has been sitting down: not mighty, learned or wise? Instead, he has become slow: slow of speech, tongue and purpose. You can almost see him trying to get up, but he just can't. At that point, he was slow and apathetic. After he ran to Midian out of a reverence for God and a holy fear to find Him, he then sat down and forgot his quest. Sweet, lonely, goodly man!

Because the excuse that he wasn't quite good enough suited him, he used it. Granted, it would be a scary, if not absolutely frightening, thing to be told by the Almighty, "I remember you were an Olympic gold medalist swimmer 40 years ago—now go jump in the water and win the race!" or, "I seem to recall that you were a brilliant surgeon 40 years ago, before your nervous breakdown—now go perform surgery on somebody." Or even, "You stood before kings and nations and commanded a kingdom with the confidence of royalty. I know you are not royalty, you are a sheepherder and have been hanging out with sheep and desert dwellers, speaking a slurred language, getting fat without a care in the world; but now I want you to go back and let Me be royalty through you. I think you are 'over yourself,' so this will work. Shall we go?"

One day, long ago, in a faraway land, Moses could speak the language and move in the culture without offending too many people. But there was no quick wit left, and his thoughts didn't form words correctly anymore. His passion had left, so he had no purpose. Why couldn't God just send somebody who could at least speak the language? *Even a slave who has been forced to understand the language would be better than me,* he must have thought. *It's been too long. How will I ever know what to do or how to do it?* Yes, these were insurmountable odds; but that seems to be the way God likes it. He loved the odds against Gideon's army, and He loved the fact that it was Noah and his family against the world. He got a huge kick out of David taking on a giant alone, and He smiles with delight at your willingness to say, "You and me, God—that's more than enough!"

He smiles with delight at your willingness to say,
"You and me, God—that's more than enough!"

Moses was trying to find a way for God to reject him. He felt unworthy and seemed to have a need to be rejected. If you feel guilty, rejected or poor, you will find ways to become guilty, rejected and poor—even if you have to sabotage yourself or set yourself up for failure to do it. The root protects itself. Moses had become well versed in finding an excuse instead of away.

God, in His abounding mercy and understanding love, tried to comfort Moses and encourage him. He didn't call him a weakling. He said to Moses that He would be with him and was able to fix any problems that might arise. God took a lot of time letting Moses know that he was accepted and not rejected. The Lord spoke to Moses in the midst of his anxiety attack and said, "Who hath made man's mouth? Or who maketh the dumb or the deaf? Or, the seeing or the blind? Have not I the Lord? Now therefore go and I will be with thy mouth and teach thee what thou shalt say." The Lord was compelling Moses to agree with Him. He was so ever-present and comforting to Moses, proclaiming to him once again who He was and what He would do for Moses; yet it still wasn't enough for Moses.

Inability to Trust
The next thing out of the mouth of Moses was a declaration of his inability to fully trust the Lord. He knew, to a greater degree that day than he did the day before, exactly who God was, but he hadn't been able to apply it to his life yet. His root of rejection was still growing branches, and the wind of opportunity was nervously blowing leaves all over him. It originally caused him to flee into a strange land and be content doing things that he was never designed to do. It had changed how Moses looked at life. He was desperate to be "normal" and not make any waves, since the last one he made had started quite a stir. But we are not called to be "normal," for the Lord has brought us to a "wealthy place" as a "peculiar people," according to the Word of God.

"Behold, the hour cometh, yea, is now come, that ye shall be scattered, every man to his own, and shall leave me alone: and yet I am not alone, because the Father is with me" (John 16:32). The

Greek word for "scattered" (*skorpizó*, #G4650) here is similar to *skorpios* (#G4651), which means, among other things, to "pierce" like a scorpion. When you become a scorpion for the sake of the Gospel, you no longer tolerate injustices around you. You are no longer afraid or bound by your insecurities and wounds. They are no longer allowed to create fears and frailties in you.

Scorpions are radical creatures! When a scorpion has its mind set on stinging you, it's hard to talk him out of it. To "scatter like a scorpion" is to penetrate the evil around you and cause it danger. In the Bible, scorpions represent danger. What evil have you been a danger to? What evil environment have you changed for His good and glory? Scorpions stand for something that is to be feared and reckoned with. Has the enemy had to reckon with you? Or is he treating you like a plain old bug? There is nothing plain about a scorpion; when you have encountered one, you remember it. Whether you've been stung or not, you remember it!

What Jesus was telling His disciples here was, "Go and get the job done. Make the enemy afraid in My name and change the face of the earth as you know it; be a scorpion!"

"Every place that the sole of your foot shall tread upon, that have I given unto you, as I said unto Moses" (Joshua 1:3).

Fear Paralyzes

The Shunamite woman in 2 Kings 4 tried to hide in a doorway and not enter in when Elisha called her. She was desperate to find a way to be "normal." Perhaps she had disappointments that were preventing her from going forward. Like Moses, she seemed to be formed by something in her past.

> ...and when he had called her, she stood in the door. And he said, About this season, according to the time of life, thou shalt embrace a son. And she said, Nay, my lord, thou man of God, do not lie unto thine handmaid. And the woman conceived and bear a son at that season that Elisha had said unto her according to the time of life.

What's with the "nay, my lord" thing? And why wouldn't she go in the room? She's got Elisha in her house. That's a big deal, and she knows it.

Elisha wasn't a quiet prophet. His ministry was very active and public. She had to have known that Elisha was powerful, yet, she could not believe. She could not trust; in fact, she didn't even want to hear it! She stood at the door, never going in, never wanting to fully embrace what was happening. The Lord overcame that woman's fear in a moment, and she became a powerful example to us all. The fear of Moses would see its death by a longer route.

Moses did the wrong thing with the information that God gave him. He let it create a lack in his life, and that lack provoked a mistake that caused him to move out of step with God, which created more rejection. The fear of living out more failure and rejection sealed the fate of this man, who was standing before his God who had chosen to pull him toward His purposes.

What you are about to read are the words of a paralyzed man. He is paralyzed with the fear of rejection. When we are paralyzed, we cannot agree with God, and His favor escapes our grasp. After the Lord gave Moses wonderful promises, reminded him that He had created all things, and told him to go and God would do all the work, Moses still said to Him, "O my Lord, send, I pray thee, by the hand of him whom thou wilt send." In other words, Moses told God, "Go ahead and find somebody else to send, because it sure isn't going to be me!"

The "I can't" thing didn't work. The "Who are You, anyway?" thing didn't work. The "Who am I, anyway?" thing didn't work. The "They won't believe me" thing didn't work. The "They'll call me a liar and say I never saw You" thing didn't work. The "I'm a lousy speaker" thing didn't work. So now, Moses gave up; but he still didn't give in. Moses rallied his emotions and, in his despair, stumbled upon a glaring truth: he just didn't want to do it. He was sure of this one thing: He couldn't and he wouldn't. He was convinced!

Moses said, "Okay, I'm out of reasons and excuses. But guess what? I'm still not doing it!"

Be careful when you start judging the will of God based upon your own fears and insecurities! As a child, I was scared to death to do what God was telling me to do. Forget that it was always a bizarre and weird thing. Forget that I was a kid and it seemed unfair. Forget that it would have been easier for someone older and wiser to do. Forget all of that, but remember this: it was what God asked me to do. So it was my job to not only find a way to do it, but also to find a way to *love* doing it!

When you are doing something for the Lord, it should look easy. There should be great joy in it, no matter what that thing is. Have you been so full of excuses of why you can't do something that you have neglected to understand the joy that will come if you do? When we are full of excuses and have no joy, then we are preventing the grace of God from fully manifesting in our lives. Grace is our ability to be Christlike in any situation. It is our inherited right and privilege to operate out of Christ's authority when we have submitted to Him and agreed with Him. When we are moving in grace, there is a joy and a peace to what we do because we are operating as an overcomer, just like Jesus did. Let grace be alive and active in your life today!

Be sure to kill all the excuses in your heart that are preventing you from agreeing with God. There is an abundant place He wants to take you to, but you can't climb that hill with all the baggage you've got strapped to your shoulders.

CHAPTER 10

Partial Obedience

And the anger of the LORD was kindled against Moses, and he said, Is not Aaron the Levite thy brother? I know that he can speak well. And also, behold, he cometh forth to meet thee: and when he seeth thee, he will be glad in his heart. And thou shalt speak unto him, and put words in his mouth: and I will be with thy mouth, and with his mouth, and will teach you what ye shall do. And he shall be thy spokesman unto the people: and he shall be, even he shall be to thee instead of a mouth, and thou shalt be to him instead of God. And thou shalt take this rod in thine hand, where-with thou shalt do signs (Exodus 4:14–17).

God is saying here, "Fine, you think it's about being a good speak-er? Your brother Aaron is a pretty good speaker—we'll get him to do it!" It was never about the ability of Moses; it was always about God's ability. God doesn't want us able—He wants us willing!

It's a dangerous thing to push God. Moses insisted that God accommodate his weaknesses. God wrestled with him, but in the end, the Lord will not force His will or desires upon us. Moses won the argument, but he would come to regret it.

One day a woman lingered around after the church service with a teenage boy. The woman was pushing the boy forward, and it annoyed me to see it. So I asked the boy who the woman was and then took him aside. He said she was his aunt. He rolled his eyes and smirked. He said that his parents were in jail and the aunt was raising him. I asked him if he wanted prayer, and he said, "No." I asked him if he had already made his mind up to do whatever he wanted in the world. He laughed and told me, very matter-of-factly, "Yes." I let him know that the Lord had set many people free that night from drug addiction, pornography, witchcraft and alcohol. I told him that they began the same way he did and pointed out where those choices had taken them. I told him that he was at the beginning of the journey and could change his destination if he wanted to. I asked, "Why go from here, run around for a decade, get a messed-up life, and then just come back to this place to get fixed up after you have bondages, regrets and torments, when you don't have to?" He just stared at me. I asked him if he was already into those things and he said, "Yes, and I like it that way."

I told him to go and know that he was loved, and when he was ready, someone would be there for him. I wept as I told him that someday he'd be back, because the Bible says that every knee will bow and every tongue confess that Jesus Christ is Lord. He grabbed my hand and said he had heard that before from his aunt. This young teenage boy thanked me, gave me a hug and left, determined in his folly and set in his ways. I prayed that the destroyer would not destroy him. Not unlike this manchild, Moses appeared to want deliverance from his own destiny.

Responding with a Passionate Faith

Second Kings 13 tells the story of the last miracle God worked through Elisha (if you don't count the one from his grave). Joash was the evil king of Israel at the time. He'd had a good upbringing, but turned from it when the priest who helped raise him died. He basically flipped out, but when he came up against hard times, he knew where to go. He went to God by way of Elisha. He had a problem and decided to behave himself long enough to get the answer. So, he went to Elisha, crying, and got him off his deathbed.

He begged Elisha for help, because the Syrians were coming to take the kingdom away from Joash.

> *And Elisha said unto him, Take bow and arrows and he took unto him bow and arrows. And he said to the King of Israel; Put thine hand upon the bow. And he put his hand upon it: Elisha put his hands upon the King's hands and he said, Open the window eastward. And he opened it. Then Elisha said, Shoot. And he shot. And he said, The arrow of the Lord's deliverance, and the arrow of deliverance from Syria; for thou shalt smite the Syrians in Aphek, till thou have consumed. And he said, Take the arrows. And he took them. And he said unto the King of Israel, Smite upon the ground. He smote thrice and stayed. The man of God was wroth with him and said, Thou shouldest have smitten five or six times; then hadst thou smitten Syria till thou hadst consumed it: whereas now thou shalt smite Syria but thrice.*

The king of Israel didn't have any passion; he just wanted to get delivered. He didn't want anything else. He took the bow and arrows and shot them out the window with some success, but when it came time to pay attention and "go for broke," Joash failed. He shot the arrows and was told, "Behold, the arrow of the Lord's deliverance!" This was the answer to his prayer; this was why he got a dying man up off his sickbed. This deserved more than a pathetic pound—it deserved a passionate one. This was to be his victory shout, his triumphant pound on the ground. But I'm afraid the king wasn't very spiritually perceptive, and he chose a weak way of responding to the provision and miracle of God, so he lost them. He was only slightly impressed by God. Was it apathy or stupidity? Maybe they are the same thing.

He was supposed to beat the Syrians beyond belief; it was to be a miracle. But instead, he only beat the Syrians according to the level of passion he displayed and the lack of belief he had hidden in his heart.

It isn't what Elisha initially spoke and it wasn't what God wanted, but it's what happened because one person decided to do it "his way." When he demanded to have it his way, he was forsaking favor. May we embrace the full move of God, not just the pieces that we are comfortable with!

In another Old Testament story, when Hezekiah was being "brought home" by the Lord, he asked for more time and let the Lord know he was not ready to die yet. He started recounting his good reputation back to the Lord, asking God to give him his way. Hezekiah argued with God at a most untimely moment. When he won his argument with God, it negatively altered the destiny of mankind. God gave him 15 more years, but they were not years of blessing—they were years of trial.

The children that were born to him during that time were evil, and his own heart gave in to pride. Earlier his testimony was spotless, but it became tarnished after he got his way. History saw the Babylonian Empire take an evil leap over Israel, because when God came calling, a man said, "Wait a minute, I've got something to say!"

Moses would learn to trust his Maker one day, but today he cried for comfort; the official cry of the people he would lead. Moses was agreeing with God, but he was doing it with reservations. He was a passionless man, moving in simple obedience that he could control. He would find out that he needed a greater mandate than an obedience that he could control to accomplish a work that would require passion, as well as compassion, to perform.

Ministering God's Love

It was a meeting that seemed to be like any other meeting—until I saw her. I was greeting people at church when I noticed someone who seemed out of place. Her name was Evelyn. She was a noticeably unkempt black woman in a predominately white, wealthy neighborhood church. As I walked over to introduce myself to her, I realized that she was blind. As I told her my name and she told me hers, I was grateful for her blindness. The smell of her body odor was beyond anything I had ever experienced. My eyes squinted as I gasped for air. I was grateful that she was unable to see me lose my composure. I found Evelyn a seat and thanked her for coming.

The worship service had begun and, as I made my way to my seat, I heard the Lord speak to my heart: "I would like to give Evelyn a hug, would you let Me do that?" "Well, of course You can, Lord!" You see, I'm a hugger from way back. I come from a long line of huggers. Hugging is good. I could hug Evelyn.

As I turned to walk in what I thought to be perfect obedience, I began to ponder Evelyn. Poor Evelyn—she was blind with no one to care for her. It seemed like she was wearing every piece of clothing that she possessed, including stray pieces of fabric that had not yet been made into clothing. All manner of stains and odor adorned this clothing. Stains derived from things inside and outside the body. Her teeth were visibly green, with things growing on them that looked like mold. Her face looked as if it had large accumulations of lard applied to it, and probably hadn't been washed for months. Poor, sweet Evelyn, with no one to care for her. I felt privileged that the Lord would entrust me with such an important job. Little did I know that my righteousness was as filthy rags.

Looking back on it, I guess I came to embrace the obedience because I figured out a way to be in control of the act of obedience. I wouldn't hug her too long or too tightly, just enough to let her know she was loved…just enough to obey…just enough to say I did it. I could stretch myself and do that. I hadn't yet learned that partial obedience is just glorified disobedience. But I would. Evelyn would teach me.

I came in behind Evelyn, put my hands on each of her shoulders and gave her a squeeze while gingerly pressing my cheek on the back of her head and said, "Oh, Evelyn, it's Sandi again. Jesus wants you to know that He loves you so very much!" Evelyn placed her hand upon one of mine and patted me. She graciously spoke, "Thank you, dear, I appreciate that." Deed done. Whew!

You did the best you could do,
now go back and do the best that I can do!

As I'm walking down the long aisle of "sanctified deeds" to my seat, I heard the Lord again, "What are you doing?" "I'm going to sit down." "No, you're not, I didn't tell *you* to hug Evelyn, I told you that *I* wanted to hug her! You did the best you could do, now go back and do the best that I can do!" What else could I do? I went to see Evelyn. Again.

There she was, in her pew. Not a living soul within ten feet of her. A seat wasn't hard to find nearby. I sat next to Evelyn. When I began to consider the bugs upon her, I determined to sit on the bugs, and I drew closer to her. Soon, my leg was pressed against hers. I said, "Evelyn, Jesus REALLY loves you!" I put both my arms around her. I went beyond a hug, beyond a squeeze, I smashed her into me, as if both our lives depended upon it, and then I put my lips upon her cheek. I gave her a kiss, a kiss that changed me. The smell was horrifying. I left my lips upon her cheek until I couldn't smell the ugliness anymore. At that point, when I lost myself in what Christ was doing, when I couldn't smell her anymore, I felt a tear, Evelyn's tear, running down over my lips. Instead of thanking me, as she had done before, she moved into what was real. She responded to the purpose of the hug.

Evelyn began to worship. She lifted her hands up as the river of her pain ran from her eyes and said, "Oh, thank You, Jesus, thank You for loving me so much and thank You for that kiss. You know, Lord, it has been almost 15 years, I suppose, since I've had a kiss. Thank You, Jesus!" She wasn't talking to me—it was Jesus. I was no longer involved; no longer a participant. She went right past me, straight to Jesus, and glorified Him. She was no longer patting my hand and simply saying thank you. As I slowly pulled away, she stood to her feet, raised both her hands and shouted praises to the Lord of Hosts!

May we live God's way so loudly that we deafen the ears of the enemy and all those who would oppose Him! Although it appeared that I lived God's heart radically that day, I did not. Evelyn did. She knew who to give the glory and adoration to. She naturally knew. I had to be convinced. As Moses walked this path, he, too, would be convinced as he learned to trust this God who was calling Him forward through time.

Just because Moses was walking toward Egypt with a mandate didn't mean he was ready to deliver it. It meant he was trusting the Lord to meet him in the middle, in spite of his inability. Moses still had conflicts, but what made him so great is that he went anyway. Even if he had to put his fears in a little wagon and drag them behind him across the desert sands of Midian all the way to Egypt, he still went! That's what bought him the privilege of shouting in Pharaoh's court, "Let the people go!"

When you look at your life, are there issues that you have avoided or just gotten by with? Maybe there was a time when you could have behaved in an abundant way; but instead, you felt you couldn't trust the Lord, so you reacted out of your own need. We can trick ourselves into thinking that we are actually doing the right thing, but it's "common and called" instead of "calculated and chosen." Awesome performance has to be planned. Plan to walk in total obedience from this day forward in whatever you set your hand and heart to do. The thing about adopting this lifestyle is that other people will come with you. They will often develop an abundant attitude right along with you. Everyone around you can change because you made a commitment toward excellence and walked away from rejection!

CHAPTER 11

Fresh or Committed

And Moses went and returned to Jethro, his father in law, and said unto him Let me go, I pray thee, and return unto my brethren which are in Egypt; and see whether they be yet alive. And Jethro said to Moses, Go in peace. And the Lord said unto Moses in Midian, Go, return into Egypt; for all the men are dead which sought thy life. And Moses took his wife and his sons, and set them upon a donkey and he returned to the land of Egypt; and Moses took the rod of God in his hand. And the Lord said unto Moses, When thou goest to return into Egypt, see that thou do all those wonders before Pharaoh, which I have put in thine hand; but I will harden his heart, that he shall not let the people go. And thou shalt say unto Pharaoh, Thus saith the Lord, Israel is my son, even my firstborn: And I say unto thee, Let my son go, that he may serve me; and if thou refuse to let him go, behold, I will slay thy son, even thy firstborn (Exodus 4:18–23).

Earlier in scripture, the Lord had told Moses the people who sought his life were now dead. It's almost as if Moses didn't hear it then, so God repeated it, knowing that Moses was finally listening because he stopped arguing with Him. When the argument is over, the wrestling clone, the decision made, we are finally in a position to hear what we wouldn't hear before. Here we have an 80-year-old man asking permission from his father-in-law to depart into the land of his forefathers. He has been tending sheep for some 40 years. They are not his sheep, but belong to his father-in-law. He has been a servant to this man, Jethro, and his reward is the identity crisis of the ages. Serving is fine, a servant's heart is important to be Christlike, but not when we use it to avoid our destiny and purpose.

"The rich rule over the poor and the borrower is servant to the lender" (Proverbs 22:7). Surely this is true in the spiritual realm, as well. When we embrace a borrowed work, we can become a slave to it. It will become drudgery in mind and conflict of soul. We will be so busy losing that we never gain. We can become trapped in it and never get out. It's just not good business to walk on another man's water.

> **He was a son whom the Father was desperate**
> **to pour out blessings of favor and abundance upon.**

Have we become servants to the service, or children in His service? Moses had not understood yet that he was a son and not a servant. He was a son whom the Father was desperate to pour out blessings of favor and abundance upon. But Moses was still wrapped up in the root of rejection and who it was dictating him to be. He would struggle until Egypt was far behind him.

> *For as many as are led by the Spirit of God, they are the sons of God. For ye have not received the spirit of bondage again to fear; but ye have received the Spirit of adoption, whereby we cry, Abba, Father. The Spirit itself beareth witness with our spirit, that we are the children of God: And if children, then heirs; heirs of God, and joint-heirs with Christ; if so be that we suffer with him, that we may be also glorified together. For I reckon that the sufferings of this present time are not worthy to be compared with the glory which shall be revealed in us* (Romans 8:14–18).

Moses had forsaken the source of disobedience and said good-bye to Midian. It wasn't that he embraced the journey or even the cause or the destination ahead; he had just forsaken the right to say "no" to God. God can work with that. While the Lord is working these things out in us, He desires to show us the difference between radical obedience and partial obedience. Partial obedience is simply glorified disobedience!

The Bloody Husband

> *And it came to pass by the way in the inn, that the Lord met him, and sought to kill him. Then Zipporah took a sharp stone and cut off the foreskin of her son, and cast it at his feet and said, Surely a bloody husband art thou to me. So He let him go; then she said, A bloody husband thou art, because of the circumcision* (Exodus 4:24–26).

Let's face it: this is some of the weirdest scripture written about the life of Moses. There is an elephant right in the middle of this story, so we might as well address it. We do not know what form God chose to take while He visited the household of Moses—whether it was an angel, a vapor or an overwhelming presence. But we do know this: it was God, and He was waiting for Moses.

As we have seen, the arguing was finally over. The conflict between man and God appeared to be settled. Moses would obey Him and go to Pharaoh. So, he packed up his wife and kids (scripture tells us he had two sons, Gershom and Eliezer), and headed off to Egypt. They stopped along the way at a little hotel for the evening and BAM! God was waiting there. He grabbed Moses and said He had come to kill him! (We know that God had a hold on Moses because, in the midst of this passage, it is written, "God let him go.")

I have a hard time believing that God would hold Moses accountable for stuff that he was unaware of. And how did Zipporah know about God's requirement of circumcision for the Israelites, anyway? She was a Midianite!

Come with me on a journey of supposition. For that is the only country we can travel through in this passage, since there isn't much explanation in scripture. However, I do feel the revelation hidden in these few words cries out to be understood.

In Exodus 18:4 it is said that "the name of the other son is Eliezer, for the God of my Father said He was my help and He delivered me from the sword of Pharaoh." We heard not a word about him, not even his name, until this passage. We know that the sons of Moses went with the family caravan on the road to Egypt, because the Word says that Moses took Zipporah and their sons. Sons is plural. So, both sons were there.

Eliezer's name means "God of help" (#H461). God was his help, his deliverer! Could it be that when good old Zipporah whipped out the rock, calling it a knife, and came after her sons to circumcise them, that Eliezer was just too quick for her? He may have thought, *Heck, man, my name means "God of help," and this thing has gone bad. I'm gonna consider myself helped and delivered!* It is only recorded that Zipporah circumcised one son. We don't hear about the sons again until Exodus 18, and then just for a moment, when they came to visit Moses with Jethro and Zipporah. The circumcision incident was really more about Moses than about Gershom or Eliezer.

Remember, these were not babies; they were grown men. Moses and Zipporah married in the first year of his Midian dwelling, and in the same breath, the Word records that she gave him children. He dwelt in Midian for 40 years. More than likely these children that Mama is coming after to circumcise with the edge of a stone are close to 40 years old!

I don't think they waited a decade to have children; it is inconsistent with both scripture and the culture and tradition of the day. Even if they waited for ten years, the men would still be almost 30 years old at the point of circumcision. They were men-children!

Moses had to have known about God's desire for His chosen people to be circumcised as a token of their heritage in God and obedience to Him, or God would not have had such a strong reaction toward their lack of circumcision. Maybe Moses was talked out of it by his sons—and why not? This was apparently not a "user-friendly" act.

During the previous few days, I'm sure that Aaron had been visiting Moses and his family quite a bit, preparing for their trip to Egypt. Aaron was probably learning how to lean on Moses as he would God, as the Lord proclaimed he should do. He was also likely learning how to handle the miraculous rod and be the spokesman that Moses was afraid to be. I'm sure they spent much time together, and it's pretty safe to say that Aaron was telling Moses, "Hey, you can't look like an Egyptian and act like a Midianite. You have to look and act like an Israelite. You have to become who you really are now. You are a Hebrew, and here is the kind of stuff that we do. These are our traditions. Here is the heart and law of the Father, whom you serve. You have to deal with the circumcision thing before we set out on our journey. We cannot have any defilement in our camp when we take on Pharaoh. If you are going to obey God, you have to obey all the way. God can't start this great work on a bad foundation of disobedience."

More than likely, Moses was willfully disregarding the command of the Lord. *What's the point of that?* he may have thought. He was 80 years old, and I'm sure circumcision wasn't an exciting option for him, either.

Moving forward for a moment, we know that Moses himself was never circumcised, because in Exodus 6:12 he says to God, "Behold the children of Israel have not hearkened unto me; how then shall Pharaoh hear me, who am of uncircumcised lips?" He says it again in Exodus 6:30 when he is speaking to the Lord: "Behold, I am of uncircumcised lips, and how shall Pharaoh hearken unto me?" He spoke these words after God tried to build his confidence and gave him specific instructions to give to Pharaoh. God was telling Moses that all He wanted was his obedient heart: "Forget about the circumcision—it's deeper than that now. Come with Me! Whatever was wrong I've made right. I forgive and accept you." But Moses was still insecure and couldn't let it go. It was over, and time to move on, but Moses was having trouble doing that just yet.

This banter continued for several long chapters. The same old invalid argument was being recycled so Moses would have the joy of feeling rejected again. You can still see him setting himself up for failure and guilt once more, succumbing to fear as if he had a mandate to be rejected and wrong.

Getting back to the Palm Inn along the Egyptian road where Zipporah is holding a sharp stone....

Protecting Those around Us

Maybe Moses couldn't hear God in this because it was just going to cost him too much, and the whole circumcision thing didn't make enough sense to an ex-Egyptian/Midianite. Maybe Zipporah was fed up with Moses and figured he was on his own, and she was going to save at least one of her sons. Maybe Zipporah knew if she circumcised her son that it would save Moses and her children. Maybe circumcising the child was enough for God, because He never required it of Moses after this point. Maybe Zipporah knew it was all about obedience. Maybe, just maybe, a lot of things.

Whatever the reason, we know that God sought to kill Moses after it appeared he had already agreed with God and was on the way to Pharaoh. That tells us that total and radical obedience didn't go very deep in Moses yet; but it would quickly arrive. Maybe he purposefully disregarded this very difficult task, figuring God would ignore it as long as he did. But God would not. It appears that God told Moses to circumcise his children, and he wouldn't do it. Zipporah had to have hidden this in her heart, waiting and watching for the fallout from Moses's decision.

Sometimes we have to protect our children when those around us have made bad decisions. God will hear you and respond to your efforts of purity and obedience toward Him. We are not held in the bondage of another if we keep pursuing Christ, keep praying and keep putting the enemy in his place—in spite of who let him in. God will always hear you. His ears have not become deaf because you are in the middle of a battle.

Imagine God, the Almighty Creator of all things, seeking you out to kill you. What a sight, what a sound, what a terror it must have been! Zipporah was a quick thinker, and it's a good thing, because we don't hear any words coming out of Moses's mouth at this point.

We've read earlier in Exodus 4 that, after Zipporah performed the circumcision, God "let Moses go." This is a dramatic picture of somebody being held with the hands of God wrapped around them. However it happened is irrelevant; the truth is that you can't let go of someone if you aren't touching them. We can only imagine what the scene looked like. This is also a powerful picture of how quickly God responds to our obedience.

The name Zipporah (#H6855) means "bird." That's all. I was hoping for some fantastic insight to help explain this phenomenal woman who wrestled her grown son to the ground, cut off his foreskin, and threw it at the feet of her husband as she saved his life. "Bird." I'm thinking hawk, eagle, pterodactyl. She doesn't strike me as a bluebird or a sparrow kind of gal. If the Israelite women were considered "lively," as we read before, I don't even want to know what the Midianite women were considered!

She said to Moses, "Surely a bloody husband thou art to me," and I imagine she was screaming that line. And she said it twice. The Bible says that she made this statement to Moses because of the circumcision. What was she talking about? The blood that the circumcision caused—the horror, the mess, the violence? No, she was yelling at Moses and blaming him for not taking care of business. This is why I think that he knew about the circumcision and made a deliberate decision to disobey God, who, by the way, was done playing this game with Moses. Moses was a "bloody husband" at this point—"bloody" is to be apathetic and to not walk in your full authority. You are guilty and will make people perish or fail around you. This word "bloody" (*dam*, #H1818) is connected to the idea that you bring with you the actual cause of death.

It is so easy to become "bloody." The people who do surveys say that we watch about 40 hours of television a week. I don't know anyone who is willing to admit to that horrible number of wasted hours, but they are out there. It's become so consuming because it's mindless entertainment. How can you advance a kingdom like that? When you are "bloody," you absolutely cannot walk in the abundant favor of God.

Moses became bloody when he was willing to ignore truth because it suited him. Sometimes, it's easier to pretend that we didn't really hear something. If it's inconvenient or inconceivable, then we can find something else to occupy our time, minds, hearts and even our wills. Being circumcised was not going to be a party, and Moses thought it best to pretend he just didn't hear God's command.

Forgetting Our True Adversary

I was in a home recently, speaking with a couple whose teenage daughter had been giving them fits. She had gone to bed and was finally sleeping after a raging outburst at her parents. They were upset and wondering what to do. I said, "That's the easy part. Let's pray and let the enemy know that he has no place in this house or in her heart; she is a child of God and, through prayer, we will overcome for her." Ephesians 6 declares, "We fight principalities and powers in high places. We don't fight flesh and blood."

It was easier for them to scream at their daughter than to take authority over the devil. When we get tired, we can forget who our true adversary is. It is the devil's great joy to get us wrapped up in fighting each other or declaring, "Oh, that's just the way it is." The "whatever spirit" is making us lazy. "What a hassle!" our body tells us. "You are too tired for that right now" we say, soothing ourselves with thoughts of nothingness. "That would take too much time— you can just pray in the car" our body pleads with us. The oldest principle that passes physical and spiritual lines is, "You get out of something only what you put into it." We've allowed ourselves to be so tired and conditioned to chasing emergencies that we don't address the truly urgent things when they come our way. Emergencies scream. Urgencies wait, but not for long. Our spiritual state is an urgent matter.

I told this couple that I'd pray with them. The wife was grateful and began to weep and say how tired she was of the fight, but that she would persevere for the sake of her daughter and to please the Lord. She trusted the Lord to give her strength. I asked the husband if he wanted to pray for a minute, and he sat looking at the television for a while and then made this startling statement to me (I'm not making this up): "Well, I don't really think I should right now. I'm kind of tired, and I think I'll just pray in the morning when I'm fresh." "Fresh?" I had to laugh at this. "Fresh?" I thought he was kidding. He had to be kidding! Surely he wasn't going to let the devil devour his daughter through the night because he was too tired to stay up and pray.

The disciples decided that not staying up to pray was a mistake when they did it, and the odds of it being a good idea now haven't increased over the years! Jesus wasn't feeling too fresh when he walked up Calvary. Jesus wasn't feeling too fresh in the Garden of Gethsemane either; He was in agony there and still continued communing with the Father. In fact, I wasn't really feeling too fresh either, but I was willing to stay and pray for their child.

"Yeah," the husband said, "I'm not feeling really fresh right now!" He got up and went to bed. I thought, *Fresh or not, this is his family and his child, and he needs to get in there and inconvenience himself and pray. Inconvenience himself in obedience to the Word of God that tells him to be the priest of his home. Inconvenience himself and scrape the devil off his child and give her the peace of God.* So, after five minutes, I asked the wife to go into the bedroom and get him. She came out teary-eyed and said he was asleep, already snoring, bloody man that he was.

The Word says that in our weakness, we are made strong. Not in our strength we are made strong. Not in our freshness—in His! Some of my most powerful times in prayer were when I would wake up in the middle of the night, coughing up blood while wracked in pain from the cystic fibrosis, pushing through to Jesus. I can't imagine that I would have grown in God at all or accomplished anything spiritual during those years if I was doped up with so much medication that I couldn't think. I had to learn to give my pain to God. We aren't allowed to simply declare that we just don't feel fresh enough to pray. The Word says to be "instant" at all times. That says to me that we are to be found fresh and ready, whether we feel like it or not. The devil isn't stupid. He isn't going to attack when you are perfectly ready. He came to the Lord in the wilderness after He was hungry, not before. May we be found being effectual and fervent to accomplish the Lord's desires down here in His time, always ready to go, pushing through our tiredness and pain. Giving it "one more mile" is the stuff of champions and heroes; that's what Jesus did. Spiritual giants maintain their frame by such exploits, and it isn't hard for them—it is second nature. Whether they are fresh or not, they yield to Christ. Grace comes alive in us when our godly behavior becomes automatic. Grace is our living ability in Christ to behave as He did.

The scary part about the "fresh man" is that he is a leader in his church and considered an awesome Christian. *This man might do something awesome once in a while, but it doesn't make him awesome!* There is a difference between being Christian and being godly, between purification and sanctification, partial obedience and radical obedience. Good is the enemy of great.

Being Ready

The Lord only tolerates disobedience and rebellion against the Spirit for so long, even when it is disguised as "our nature or character or gift," and then He comes seeking to "kill it." Death in the Spirit is a terrible and ugly thing to watch. The Lord will not let you carry the mantle of His power when you are "bloody." This is not about *acting* ready, but about *being* ready. This is not about salvation; it is about sanctification. The Lord loves us too much to leave us the way we are. The greatest lesson Moses would learn about being a man was obedience, and he just learned it!

It seems like obedience is a lifelong lesson that we figure out in one form and then have to learn it again in another form. We get the date right and the time is wrong, or we get the time right and we are standing in the wrong location! Sometimes it's because we are willful, and other times it's because we have become unable to pay attention to the important signs around us. Either way, it's what God calls "Egypt," and it has to go!

The Israelite nation encamped at Gilgal so they could be circumcised before the battle. "And the LORD said unto Joshua, This day have I rolled away the reproach of Egypt from off you. Wherefore the name of the place is called Gilgal unto this day" (Joshua 5:9).

This was a point of purifying their hearts and minds. This would "get Egypt out of them" and cause them to succeed. The circumcision here, just as it was for Moses earlier and the teachings of Paul the apostle later, was about the heart. What were they willing to believe God for? Would they be willing to get past themselves in order to believe it, or would they simply, easily act like Egyptians?

Sometimes life is simpler when we are just Egyptians, isn't it? Simple and slow and, well, too simple.

The obedience that Moses was walking in at this point wasn't exactly "reckless abandon," but nevertheless, it was obedience. His manhood wouldn't provoke him tomorrow as much as it did today. He would walk forward, limping at times, staggering a bit, but he would not go backward; and that holds great value when we are working out the rules on how to become a vessel of God.

CHAPTER 12

Meekness—God's Way

And the Lord said to Aaron, Go into the wilderness to meet Moses. And he went, and met him in the mount of God, and kissed him. And Moses told Aaron all the words of the Lord who had sent him, and all the signs which he had commanded him. And Moses and Aaron went and gathered together all the elders of the children of Israel: And Aaron spake all the words which the Lord had spoken unto Moses, and did the signs in the sight of the people. And the people believed: and when they heard that the Lord had visited the children of Israel, and that he had looked upon their affliction, then they bowed their heads and worshipped (Exodus 4:27–31).

It is here that the man of God would determine how intently he would become the vessel of God and leave his manhood behind. It is here, looming in the shadow of Pharaoh's court, that he must decide if he would be a mere man or an honored vessel. In order to become a true vessel of God, we must rid ourselves of fears, haunts of failures and insecurities. If not, those attributes of evil will dominate and manipulate the ministry and the call the Lord has set before us and eventually destroy the true work of power and purity the Lord intends. As we have discovered, there are many wounds that attempt to hold us captive, but the fear of rejection is often leading the assault against our freedom. Just as Paul told Timothy in 2 Timothy 2:19–26, Moses would also learn the value of forsaking his manhood for obedience.

> *Nevertheless the foundation of God standeth sure, having this seal, The Lord knoweth them that are His. And, let every one that nameth the name of Christ depart from iniquity. But in a great house there are not only vessels of gold and of silver, but also of wood and of earth; and some to honour, and some to dishonour. If a man therefore purge himself from these, he shall be a vessel unto honour, sanctified, and meet for the master's use, and prepared unto every good work. Flee also youthful lusts: but follow righteousness, faith, charity, peace, with them that call on the Lord out of a pure heart. But foolish and unlearned questions avoid, knowing that they do gender strifes. And the servant of the Lord must not strive; but be gentle unto all men, apt to teach, patient. In meekness instructing those that oppose themselves; if God peradventure will give them repentance to the acknowledging of the truth; And that they may recover themselves out of the snare of the devil, who are taken captive by him at his will.*

Paul told Timothy that "God knows those that are His." He knows you and what He has designed you to do. At the end of this passage in 2 Timothy, Paul further tells Timothy that he must be the kind of man who is able to help someone who will not help themselves. He must be the kind of man who is willing to teach the truth with peace and power. They have to be taught with the greatest of love and patience so they can come to the understanding that God will never give up on them. Paul is telling Timothy that he can't "get sick" of the weak people, he has to protect and guide them with patience. (The Word further says we must "uphold the weak.")

Meekness
The "meekness" mentioned here in 2 Timothy, as Paul describes it, is the kind of meekness required for Christian service. Its root

word *praus* (#G4239) means to be "mild" and "humble." As we shall see, this is a completely different "meek" than the "meek" used to describe Moses! In the end, Moses would change his revelation of "meekness" and embrace Paul's. One would handicap him; the other would empower him.

There is one small problem with Moses at this point, and it concerns his character. It is a problem that God would immensely use to His benefit later and turn into one of his best character traits, but for now, it is a problem. And we can see by review, it has been the basis for most of the trouble Moses had at the burning bush. It was the basis for his apathy about the circumcision, and he wasn't born with it. It evolved down through the years after his identity was handed down from mother to mother. It was refined in error when his kinsmen rejected him. It developed as a handicap while his rejection produced insecurity.

Numbers 12:3 states, "Now the man Moses was very meek, above all the men which were upon the face of the earth." This word "meek" (*anav*, #H6035) means "depressed…in mind (gentle)… (needy…) – humble, lowly, meek, poor." He was depressed and considered needy. What has formed and developed you while you weren't looking?

All of a sudden the exchanges in Exodus 3 and 4 make sense. This does not appear to be a recipe for the character of someone who would go to Pharaoh and make demands in the name of God. But yet, here is God, "confounding the world with His wisdom…." So, it isn't that God was going to work through Moses because he was a motivating, confident, assuring individual. God picked the most unlikely candidate. This is the guy whose knees would be knocking as he approached Pharaoh's ominous throne. This is the guy who would cry all the way to the castle and probably have to deal with bladder control. Moses, the man who was a bit depressed and very needy, was the vessel God would move through to perform spectacular exploits. The Lord wasn't going to move through Moses because of who he was, but in spite of who he was. God was saying in essence, "Watch what I can do!" The Word says in Daniel, "Those who know their God will do exploits…." Oh, that we would know

Him! This is not a Word just for this man, but for every man, woman and child who would dare to believe that God is bigger than they are and that they were created for a divine purpose, designed by the Master, and fit for His use.

The Lord wasn't going to move through Moses because of who he was, but in spite of who he was.

God would make the man a vessel of honor whom He could truly move through with power, and in the end, call him friend. If God had such high plans for a man like Moses, then there is hope for us.

The "meekness" of Moses, which was formed by the world, as we have read, is traced back to a word (*anah*, #H6031) that means "to depress…weaken." When Moses left Midian, he left in his weaknesses. The goal was to lose his kingdom and gain God's. It would be a journey he would suffer to take and live to enjoy; but for now, he was moving ever so softly. He became every man in Midian; he became you and me. Aaron was in the lead. He moved forward with words and deeds in the sight of the people. Because of the miracles in the hands of Aaron, the people believed. They believed because of what they saw, not because of what they knew, and this attitude would cost them their promise in the end.

It is to the credit of Moses that he was going. Afraid and almost feeble minded, insecure in his abilities, rejected by men and from time to time depressed; but he was going. It is amazing to consider what Moses has overcome just to get to the palace once again.

The behavior Moses employed way back in Egypt all those years before was the opposite of his behavior on the mountain in Midian, when he was indecisive and unsure. This was not the man "who was not afraid of the wrath of the king" so he killed and buried an Egyptian. When he allowed rejection to produce insecurities and fears, he submitted to it. When he heard the enemy's voice above God's, he allowed himself to be "taken at the will of the enemy." Unknowingly, Moses gave the enemy permission to manipulate his God-given character and nature. Who and what you submit to becomes binding upon you. If we don't submit to God's authority, we can't walk in His authority. Likewise, when we do submit to God's authority, all His authority becomes ours.

Moses allowed the weakest part of himself to become the strongest. His "gifts" were being used against him. The Lord said, "In your weakness, I am made strong." He was speaking of allowing who He is to overcome our weaknesses. But Moses had allowed his weaknesses to be overcome by the root of rejection that held him captive, instead of God. He then became negatively empowered by the fear that it produced. He was so meek that it was overwhelming, and he could barely make a decision without the help of another. He could barely pick his head up and couldn't discern what to do most of the time. He was needy and emotionally afflicted. He didn't start out this way, but he ended up this way. In the end, his meekness would be his greatest quality—a necessary and essential ingredient to be a friend of God. But that day, it was attempting to paralyze him. Moses would have to learn to walk in God's empowering meekness and not man's handicapping meekness.

When we allow our gifts to lead us, then we can no longer hear the Lord clearly, for we are being guided by our gifts and not our Lord. For instance, take the gift of mercy. Now, this is a great gift, but when used by man and not the Lord, this gift can allow the enemy to destroy the person who carries it. It will cause them to rarely fight or stand passionately to advance or defend a cause. The devil intimidates them by saying that they shouldn't offend anyone or cause any "trouble." Mercy dictated out of the fear of rejection and insecurity can kill a righteous cause. Showing mercy and being merciful are different things, and we should know how to operate in those differences. "Showing it" is giving it when it is needed; "being it" is not being able to respond any other way. A mighty warrior can show mercy if he is full of God. But if the mighty warrior is consumed only by mercy, he will never get up and fight. Too often, we let one gift overcome and overwhelm us so that we become the gift and no longer resemble the giver of the gift. We can get our identity from the gift and not Jesus, and that is when we become a liability in the middle of our giftedness.

However, mercy given as a gift from God and protected under the power and purity of the Lord is a gift that goes forward with passion, accomplishing great things for the Lord and protecting the weak, not lending itself to judgment or becoming weak itself. True mercy will kill if it has to in order to protect the purity and plan of God. Yes, even in the name of mercy. The devil loves to cause mercy to be misunderstood. So, many people with this gift become backward, unwilling and unable to fight for justice. They become apathetic and tired, revolting against battle, any kind of battle. We need mercy shown, but not to the enemy or his plots, only to those who have been trapped by them. Then the mercy is given in order to bring them up out of their captivity, not lull them to sleep in it.

I love peace, but I understand that we often have to go to war to secure that peace. In the physical and spiritual realms, the law is no different in that regard. Not all things can be negotiated.

Letting His Light Shine
The devil has a whole generation of godly, merciful people who are convinced that doing the right thing would be unmerciful because they are following their gift and not the Lord. Most any gift has the potential for good or bad. The Lord won't take those gifts away; He expects us to be responsible with them and allow *His* light to shine through them, not *our* light. Are you a worshipper that worships worship? A warrior that worships and seeks out a war? A teacher that worships teaching and has forsaken the supernatural, unexplainable things of God? Allowing our gifts to become "bloody" will turn us into cowards who are afraid of the truth.

Moses lost himself in the cure and now he would have to find God in order to find himself again. This time, he would find himself as a godly vessel of honor, not just a man. He would eventually forsake his brand of meekness for the kind of meekness that Paul was telling Timothy about. He was meek to his dismay now, but under God's direction and empowerment, it would become the best part of his nature: he would become humble with a humility that had no strings. True humility is not only willing to be laid low, but it is willing to lift another up. Soon, Moses would walk that out.

Have you been so "meek" that it has handicapped you beyond ability? Sometimes our nature can do that to us. Take inventory of "who you are" right now and find out if that person is in the way of God's plans and desires for you. When we lend ourselves to depression, we cannot pick anyone else up out of it. It's scary to trust God with those things that provoke our minds, but to be a vessel, you must let Him heal your mind and emotions. As a vessel of God, we have to be thinking clearly and completely whole. We cannot be altered by external things that were created to temper or control our emotions; we have to be whole and trust the Lord to live through those emotions and heal them. As you give control of your life to Jesus and begin to trust Him, you will find that you are not nearly as depressed and rejected as you thought! You will discover that, in fact, you are a creation of the Almighty, fit to be His friend by becoming a vessel operating only unto Him and nobody or nothing else. Trust Jesus today to take control as you lose control to Him. Because truly, we don't need any new *definitions* of the Gospel, but we desperately need a fresh *demonstration* of the power of the Gospel.

Making Midian a memory isn't easy. Our hearts will pound as we venture toward redemption from all those things that have held us in their grip. We must persevere, believing in the One who has made a way for us to walk in freedom.

Moses has met the God of creation and commits to follow Him. As he leaves his manhood behind and moves forward to the likeness of his God, I can imagine him searching his soul and finding these words of offering welling up from within:

> Lord, You have destroyed the fear and rejection that has caused me to need control and kept me from leaning on You. Now I know that I am no longer rejected; I am accepted. I deny the curse that has been upon my life because of my need for identity in anything other than

You. I will no longer be controlled by the past, but go forward into the future. I forgive those who planted the seeds of rejection in me, and I ask You to bless them, heal them and deliver them. Lord, make me a vessel of honor for Your glory. Amen.

From the Plagues to the Promises

The Difference between Faith and Trust

CHAPTER 13

Obedience Can Be Hard

Truth is only relevant to those who are willing to hear it. When we declare from the mountaintop that "things are going to change," and we attempt to implement a new way of doing things, often we will be met with opposition for our attempt to walk in obedience.

Living in abundance comes with a price. If that price is truth, we must pay it and "press on toward the goal of the prize of the upward call of God in Jesus Christ" (Philippians 3:14). However, when our truth and quest for obedience begin to demand something of others, they may have something to say about it. Nevertheless, God's abundance is right on the other side of our obedience!

> *And afterward Moses and Aaron went in, and told Pharaoh, Thus saith the Lord God of Israel, Let my people go, that they may hold a feast unto me in the wilderness. And Pharaoh said, Who is the Lord that I should obey his voice to let Israel go? I know not the Lord, neither will I let Israel go. And they said, The God of the Hebrews hath met with us: let us go, we pray thee, three days' journey into the desert and sacrifice unto the Lord our God; lest he fall upon us with the pestilence, or with the sword. And the King of Egypt said unto them, Wherefore do ye, Moses and Aaron, let the people from their works? Get you unto your burdens (Exodus 5:1–4).*

In the verses above, Pharaoh was saying that he didn't know God and didn't really care about Him or the Israelites. "Who are you guys that you can tell me and my workers what to do? Go take care of your own business and leave mine alone!" His attitude is the attitude of the world toward the desires of God: selfish, stubborn, arrogant and independent. Pharaoh, just as the world, must come to see his need for God.

Pharaoh was threatened, and he turned that threat into punishment upon the people. Threatened people punish the source of the threat in hopes that it never rises up to challenge them again. Intimidation bathed in fear is terrible, but when it is given power, it can be deadly. Pharaoh had become deadly.

"So the people were scattered abroad throughout all the land of Egypt to gather stubble instead of straw" (Exodus 5:12). Pharaoh continued to proclaim his power over the people and said that because Moses and Aaron had the nerve to command the people's freedom, even just for three short days, and to fill their heads with silly notions of allowing them "rest from their burdens," he would now cause them pain. Pharaoh told the taskmasters to make them work harder by not letting them talk and withholding the straw to mix with the mud to make the bricks. Nevertheless, they still had to meet their daily quota of bricks, even though they would have to find stubble from all over Egypt and bring it back to make the bricks. If their quota of bricks was not met, he told the taskmasters to beat the Israelite officers.

These "officers" were men from the Israelite camp whom Pharaoh had placed in leadership positions over the other Israelites—kind of a "prison trustee" position. Imagine the horror of seeing your people punished and knowing you can do nothing to help. Then imagine the terror of knowing that if they fail, you are going to be beaten yourself, over and over again! Arguing and murmuring would abound in such an environment, and Pharaoh planned it that way.

When the officers went to Pharaoh to complain about how badly they were being beaten and how unfair it was that they had to use stubble instead of straw to make bricks, Pharaoh told them it was their own fault. He said they were too idle and obviously didn't have enough to do, since they had time on their hands to go sacrifice to the Lord. So the officers lost their case before Pharaoh and were told to get back to work and not be short one brick. In Exodus 5:19 it says, "And the officers of the children of Israel did see that they were in evil case." In other words, they knew that they were done for. There was no favor from Pharaoh to be had. They couldn't come against Pharaoh, so they would come against Moses instead.

Making bricks with no straw is a tough mandate. Sometimes life commands us to "make bricks without straw." It's during those times that we must remember the words of Paul in 2 Corinthians 4, "We are troubled on every side, yet not distressed; we are perplexed, but not in despair; persecuted, but not forsaken; cast down, but not destroyed." We simply have to choose what we believe in: destruction or life. No matter what life looks like, if we have chosen life in Christ, He will make our days abundant, even if that life has disguised itself to look like destruction. When the world throws "stubble" our way, we must hold onto the truth that the Holy Spirit has deposited in us!

In Daniel 6, after Daniel received the favor from the king, only then was he thrown into the lions' den. In John 11, there were lots of friends present at the funeral of Lazarus. Jewish leaders were in attendance to pay their respects as well. Lazarus must have been important, but when he was raised from the dead, he lost a lot of those "friends." After his resurrection, the Pharisees sought to kill Lazarus. (Probably the same guys who brought potato salad to his funeral and spoke about what a great guy he was.) Once you are raised from the dead, things change. Sometimes you offend people with your passion. But we can't let people's words or deeds bring about the death of our spirit. Lazarus had a passion after he rose from the dead that he didn't have before. He had a message and a purpose, and it caused anger in the people who had none. We shouldn't hang out with those people. We need to walk with Jesus, who has called us up out of the grave of rejection and fear.

*We need to walk with Jesus, who has called us up
out of the grave of rejection and fear.*

The Israelites needed this message. In spite of what Pharaoh said, they should have continued believing what they had believed earlier. Remember? When the miracles were done in their camp by Aaron, they believed! But it wasn't a believing that was birthed out of fellowship with God—it was mere relationship. "I will follow You because of what You can do for me." In their hearts they followed Him for what they could get instead of what they could give. One is the attitude of a servant, the other of a son. One is the heart of a slave, the other of an heir. One is the attitude of the multitude and the other should be the church. When the going got tough, they forgot who they were and what they believed.

Acceptance of the Promise

This next set of circumstances would forever define who Israel had chosen to be.

> *And they met Moses and Aaron, who stood in the way, as they came forth from Pharaoh: And they said unto them, The Lord look upon you, and judge; because ye have made our savour to be abhorred in the eyes of Pharaoh, and in the eyes of his servants, to put a sword in their hand to slay us. And Moses returned unto the Lord, and said, Lord, wherefore hast thou so evil entreated this people? Why is it that thou hast sent me? For since I came to Pharaoh to speak in thy name, he hath done evil to this people; neither hast thou delivered thy people at all* (Exodus 5:20–23).

The promise of deliverance is one thing; Israel's acceptance of that promise is quite another. They understood what they would be delivered out of, but they weren't absolutely sure of what they would be delivered into! They probably had a good idea of the joy that awaited them, but they were oblivious to the cost it would take to walk in that provision and promise.

The people were telling Moses, "Pharaoh has never hated us like this before. He can't stand the sight or smell of us now, and it's your fault!" They began asking God to judge Moses and Aaron for the awful tragedy that Pharaoh didn't like them anymore. God was separating them from Egypt and from their sin. We don't always like that. People pleasers will always be at war with God.

We need to hold on against the odds, the negative flow and the bad reports. Just because it doesn't look good doesn't mean it isn't good. Just because we don't hear what we want to hear doesn't mean that we haven't heard God.

Remember earlier, the Lord told Moses that Pharaoh would not believe him and that God Himself would "harden Pharaoh's heart" so that he would not let the people go. Losing sight of that statement caused Moses some grief. So the hardening of Pharaoh's heart was God's answer to a prayer, a fulfillment of a promise, a prophetic truth coming to pass. Pharaoh's heart was hardening, and in the process, he would come to hate all that was godly around him, and surprisingly, this is good. It means that God has not forgotten, and He is working on the deliverance!

Moses went to God and gave Him the "What are You doing anyway?" speech. I absolutely love God's response to Moses, for it is the same truth today as it was then. What is the answer when we have trouble? What is the answer when life is unfaithful and horrible? What is the answer when it seems that the Lord has forgotten us and life is beating hard upon us? The answer was the same for Moses as it is for us today. After Moses declares to God that "it sure doesn't seem like You are delivering anybody," in Exodus 6, God makes the declaration of the ages back to Moses: "I AM THE LORD!" That's it. That's enough. That'll do it! That's what the Lord shouts to our troubles too. That's what He declares over our lives and hearts. This amazing statement is all the defense that we will ever need. The great I AM is looking out for us. He tells our troubles and afflictions to beware because HE IS THE LORD and He's on His child's side, looking out for them.

The Dream
This past year, while I was in India on a ministry trip, a strange thing

happened. One of the team members had a dream that I got a new car. What a silly dream! We should be dreaming about saving the Muslims and Hindus, right? Well, he felt dumb, so he didn't say anything. But he had the dream for two nights in a row, and then on the third night, we both had the same dream. He couldn't stand it anymore. So early the next morning, he pulled me aside and told me about this "stupid" dream that he couldn't shake. The interesting thing about it was that the dream I had was exactly the same as his. We compared notes and colors. Everything was the same. There was this guy with black hair who had this new, brown Chevrolet Tahoe, and he was going to give it to me. (Surprisingly enough, a man that I knew did, in fact, have a new, brown Chevy Tahoe!)

When I started preaching, I gave up my "cool cars." Now, I was driving this 18-year-old "classic" (as I called it). But I really needed a newer car. This one wasn't going to last much longer. Still, I kept that knowledge to myself.

So this man (who had the dream) and I agreed in prayer, "Yep, I'm getting me a brown Tahoe—thanks, Lord!" We held onto that dream, believing that it was prophetic and it was God's desire. A couple weeks later, our team returned to the United States. When I arrived home, there was no brown Tahoe in my driveway. But that was okay, because I knew that the brown Tahoe man was going to be at a meeting that I was also attending a couple of weeks later. *So, hey,* I thought, *he'll probably just give me the brown Tahoe then.*

I went to the meeting, and the guy was there. He was so excited and came running over to me. He said, "I'm glad to see you back! A strange thing happened to me while you were gone. A few weeks ago, I had this dream about you. Funny thing is, I had this dream for a whole week and couldn't shake it. You know that nice, brown Tahoe that I bought a couple months ago?"

I smiled. "Yes?"

"Well," he continued, "I had a dream that I was supposed to give that car to you."

"Oh, really?" I said.

"Yeah, but then I realized that it wasn't God telling me that, because He would want you to have something way nicer than that car!" He went on to tell me that he ended up giving the Tahoe to someone else, and bought himself another new car. That guy stole my brown Tahoe, just like that!

God will have His way, in spite of people. We kept praying for the vehicle, knowing we had heard God. I wasn't praying for a car before this time because it just wasn't part of my thought process. I didn't care about getting a new car before the dream, before "God said!" My car was running okay for the time being. But when the dream came, I knew what God wanted to do, and it was my responsibility to agree with God and pray it in. That takes time and effort, and sometimes we can get discouraged because it seems like it will never come. If we are not careful, this is the place where we can begin to question whether we really heard God or not. But we must hold onto His promises.

It took a little longer to get here, but it came! Almost exactly a year to the date later, someone gave me a car twice as nice as the brown Tahoe. One man heard God and disobeyed; another man heard God and obeyed. Through it all, my promise never changed. I was merely given more time to worship the Lord on this side of the Red Sea in that great land called "The Waiting!"

Keep Believing

Often the word or promise itself will come to "try" you and ask the question, "Do you really believe?" The Shunammite in 2 Kings 4 had this "trying time," and knew how to hold on. She protested to Elisha that she didn't want a child and just wanted to be left alone. Sometimes we get weary of believing and refuse the avenue that will teach us hope. This woman tried to take that path, but the prophet wouldn't let her! Elisha prayed a promise over her anyway, and within a year, she had a baby boy. When the child died, she marched right over to Elisha and ordered him to bring the child back. She said, "I didn't ask for this child—you gave him to me. And now, you are going to fix this mess!" She had confidence in what God would do for her, based upon two things: her belief in the power of God and her knowledge of God's plan for her.

This information allowed her to fight death and win, because she knew both what she believed, and in whom she believed. When you are armed with that kind of ammunition, there is no battle that you cannot win, there is no truth you do not understand, and no cause given by God that you will not submit to.

In spite of Pharaoh, Israel must have believed that the great I AM was on the job, even if Pharaoh was stealing their "brown Chevy Tahoe." The world will always try to get you to doubt God. The Lord will always try to get you to believe Him, and the enemy will always try to get you to think the Lord is not looking out for you.

What is our portion in all of this? John says that "if we believe, we shall see the glory of God." But how do I believe? Most of the "believes" (*pisteuó*, #G4100) in the gospels mean that we "put" our "trust" in Christ. And the word "believe" comes from a word (*pistis*, #G4102) in the original Greek that means "credence, moral conviction (of religious truth)…constancy in such profession…faith." Without faith, I cannot trust and believe. To get faith, I must read the Word of God (as Romans 10:17 says, "Faith cometh by hearing and hearing by the word of God.") To read the Bible in a way that will change my life, I have to have a love for the Lord and His Word. Galatians 5 says that love activates faith and makes it work. So faith becomes a love issue. True love will trust.

It is the "no matter what" kind of trust. It's the kind of trust that runs to be proven and tried–it embraces the process. To truly obey God on the deepest of levels, He has to be the object of our obedience, and we have to believe that He is trustworthy.

When bad things happen, it's sometimes hard to reconcile our faith with our circumstances. When we have trusted the Lord to take care of something and it appears that He has failed because of the tragedy that now lies at our feet, what do we do? It comes down to believing, doesn't it? We must believe that He Is. No matter what it looks like, He Is.

If you are in the middle of a mess and feel like you cannot trust the Lord, then I ask you to look inside yourself. Perhaps there was a prompting of the Holy Spirit and you missed it, or someone else missed it for you. Perhaps the Lord was trying to talk to you, and you missed Him. Maybe it didn't have to end up that way, but somebody got willful and it changed the course of your history. God is still in charge of your destiny. Trust is a tough mandate when it comes calling if your faith is still shaking, but nevertheless, you have to dare to believe again.

Blessed is she that believed: for there shall be a performance of those things which were told her from the Lord (Luke 1:45).

CHAPTER 14

Unable but Willing

And I will harden Pharaoh's heart, and multiply my signs and my wonders in the land of Egypt (Exodus 7:3).

God proceeded to tell Moses that He had a plan, a perfect plan that would show His hand in a greater way. God would harden Pharaoh's heart!

In Exodus 6:30, Moses had just announced to the Lord, "Behold, I am of uncircumcised lips, and how shall Pharaoh hearken unto me?" He graduated from worrying about the people believing him to worrying about Pharaoh believing him. This seems like progress, but I'm not sure. Either way, God was not inclined to spend much time convincing Moses this time. In Exodus 7, God simply told Moses that He would be with him and that the Lord had made him to be as a god to Pharaoh. He let Moses know that Aaron would be there if he needed him, but he, most assuredly, was going on this journey with God. Again, I'm not sure if this is good or bad, but the time to figure things out was over. This is the point of no return for Moses. He was willing to believe but convinced that he was not able. This is the position that every vessel of God must be in: the position of impending perfection.

Forty years in the desert was supposed to prepare Moses. Ready or not, it was time! When you graduate from the school of brain surgery, it's not a good idea to perform surgery on people's feet.

When you graduate from school, people won't understand if you say that you just aren't prepared. It's time to perform, remember? You graduated! Whether Pharaoh was ready to believe Moses or not didn't matter. It was time to storm the palace.

So the Lord "hardened Pharaoh's heart" in order to show Himself strong. Has the Lord hardened your situation so that He can multiply His signs and wonders upon you? It can be the worst of times and the best of times, all at the same time! Sickness, persecution, poverty, and the destruction of relationships are never any fun; but if we respond correctly, seeking God's heart and not deliverance, we shall surely rise up in the midst of this "hardening" as soft clay in the potter's hand.

As they stood in Pharaoh's court, Pharaoh asked for a sign. Aaron gave him one by throwing his rod down in front of Pharaoh and watched as it became a serpent. As vessels of God, as people who are willing to allow the Lord to move through us and show Himself strong to others, it's important that we understand this lesson above all others: *It's our job to obey, and God's job to perform the object of that obedience.* It doesn't matter what it looks like or when it comes; if we've heard God, we've heard God, and that should always be enough!

"Faith is the substance of things hoped for, the evidence of things not seen" (Hebrews 11:1). Trust! In other words, Faith is the assurance of receiving the things that you are hoping for. You already know that they are coming, so you don't need to fret over them or even see them! But the confidence to walk in that faith starts with knowing that you are hoping for what God is hoping for.

Back at the palace, we seem to have an abundance of snakes crawling around now. When you throw your rod down before Pharaoh, it's all over for you at that point; God is either in it or He's not. Something supernatural will happen or it won't. Aaron's rod turned into a snake, and Moses must have let out a sigh of relief. He was convinced but not committed, so the ground beneath him still shook. When you're waiting on a miracle, sometimes there are earthquakes.

The last time Moses threw something down in the name of God, it didn't go too well. A dead Egyptian lay at his feet, his own people (past, present and future) turned on him, and God didn't rescue him, so he ran. Would he run again now, or stand and let God work it out? Aaron was beside him and God was in front of him, but I imagine that Moses was still shaking at this point.

Another Opportunity

Then, the thing that brought delight to God and horror to the heart of Moses happened next: the magicians came! Another opportunity for God to show Himself strong had come upon Egypt. With God's snake crawling around before the throne of Pharaoh, it's easy to believe we are on the winning side. But what happens when our snake is outnumbered, and a seemingly greater miracle appears at the hand of our adversary? Well, that's when we wait. Yes, looking right in the face of a potential snakebite, we wait! As the Lord pulls our fears and insecurities out of us, the world is ready and willing to shove them back in. We must guard our hearts from every evil work and simply stand and wait on our God.

Pharaoh called for all his wise men and sorcerers to take care of the snake that God had produced. "For they [the magicians] cast down every man his rod, and they became serpents...." (Exodus 7:12). At that point, I wonder what the heart rate for Moses was. Imagine the drama of it all. As the magicians marched in and threw their rods down, the human mind must have reconciled all the possibilities as it fought with faith. As the magicians' rods turned into snakes, Moses must have pondered his "last words," and recited his speech to himself about his unworthy, uncircumcised lips. "Great," he must have quivered inside, "Now Pharaoh is really not going to believe me!"

When you are waiting for redemption,
a moment can truly seem like a lifetime!

God will go to any length to accomplish His causes and reveal His purposes if we just hold on. The Word has already told us, in

Ephesians 6, that when we've done everything else (obeyed) and there is nothing left to do, we need to just stand. This is the position in which Moses found himself. He was simply standing there with a bunch of snakes crawling around at his feet, waiting on God. That is a creepy situation—unnerving, to say the least. You had to know that these snakes had one thing in mind, and that was to scare the life out of Moses. How long they crawled around we do not know. When you are waiting for redemption, a moment can truly seem like a lifetime!

Then it happened:

> *For they cast down every man his rod, and they became serpents: but Aaron's rod swallowed up their rods. And he hardened Pharaoh's heart, that he hearkened not unto them; as the Lord had said* (Exodus 7:12–13).

God won the battle, and Pharaoh was mad—really mad. In the midst of the raging war, Moses learned that no matter what the circumstances looked like, God was still bigger than all that surrounded him. When a pharaoh rises up in our own lives with an angry tirade, we have to know if we heard God or not. Because Pharaoh will know if we haven't really heard; he'll know if we are kidding ourselves. He'll know by the sweat on our brow and the quiver in our voice. Therefore, without a doubt, we must take time to learn how to "know."

It's important to note that, in all of this, God was not moving through Moses, but through Aaron. Moses was just watching and learning to trust. As a vessel of God, we must come to the place of trust; for without that, we will never be able to stand when the snakes are crawling around our feet. When we are wounded, we cannot trust; we can only worry about getting bit, because we vividly remember the pain.

> *And the Lord said unto Moses, Pharaoh's heart is hardened, he refuseth to let the people go. Get thee unto Pharaoh in the morning; lo, he goeth out unto the water; and thou*

shalt stand by the river's brink against he come; and the rod which was turned to a serpent shalt thou take in thine hand (Exodus 7:14–15).

Often our difficulties are allowed to prepare us to see God's glory. Trials refine us and allow the soil of our heart to produce good fruit. When your brown Chevy Tahoe drives away, are you going to shout, "Glory to God, something better is on the way!" or will it be, "God is unfaithful and unfair"? Trust will shout one thing; fear and insecurity will shout another. The statements you make during your trials will help determine the outcome beyond those trials. Through these trials, you will learn to show—by your heart and behavior—who you know Christ to be in you. We are learning and growing, but we are also teaching the enemy what he can and cannot do with us.

Another Lesson

I'm not sure if Moses shared God's excitement about the fact that Pharaoh's heart was hardened or not; but either way, another lesson lay at his feet. God told Moses to go meet Pharaoh in the morning and take Aaron with him. Then, God told Moses to tell Aaron to stretch his rod out over the waters in front of Pharaoh, and He would turn the rivers into blood. The water would stink, and fish would die. "Take Aaron. Tell Aaron. Take Aaron. Tell Aaron." Someday other words would be spoken; but for now, God was finding a way to make it work for Moses.

The Lord went a bit further and told Moses to have Aaron proclaim these things over the ponds, streams and pools of water as well—even over the water that was carried in vessels of wood and stone. The Word of God says that, throughout Egypt, the land smelled and the people couldn't drink because the Lord had turned their water into blood.

Then the declaration of the stupidity of pride arrives. The magicians, who never seemed to be far from Pharaoh, decided to show what they could do. So the Bible says they used "enchantments" upon what little water there was left and turned it into blood as well. For seven days, the Egyptians had no water. Sometimes we can be so overcome with wanting to prove a point that we lose track of the eternally fatal consequences looming off in the distance as a reward for our willfulness.

God then gave Pharaoh another warning. He said "Look—let My people go or I'm going to infest this place with frogs. The frogs will come up out of the river and live in your ovens and your houses and beds and will be all over the people." But Pharaoh didn't care. So, here came the frogs! And, once again, beyond all reason and at any cost, the magicians were ready to prove a point. So they conjured up some frogs of their own, as if there weren't enough frogs already! For some of us, it's easier to push our own way through in pride and get more frogs than to repent and watch God deliver us from the frogs that already exist.

Pharaoh now begged God to remove the frogs; he promised to behave himself and let the people go. God did, but Pharaoh did not! As a true testimony of God's desire and ability to bail us out of the trouble we create for ourselves, He not only delivers them from the frogs they earned by their disobedience, but He also throws in a rescue mission because of the frogs they created themselves! Aaron was still the vehicle through which God performed these things, but Moses carried the mandate of God. And somehow, God was patient enough to wait on this man who would someday be His friend. Moses was convinced of the power of God, but not yet committed to his own purposes within it. Moses cried to the Lord to remove the frogs because Pharaoh asked him to. He was learning the ways of God, but had not yet understood that a declaration of God cannot be dictated by a man—no matter who that man is!

I think we've all been there. Maybe it's spiritual peer pressure, or maybe it's pride. When people want something badly enough, they can provoke us to pray for what they want and not necessarily what God wants. It's our job to know what God is telling us to do. Everyone has their own portion as a vessel of God. One may believe for this and another for that. But what is your portion? That is the only thing God will hold you accountable for—the thing you are supposed to know. Zipporah won't always be around to save you! We must defend the honor and cause of Christ in us because nobody else is going to.

It's monumental that Moses was asking God for a miracle. And God heard it, for in Exodus 8:13 we have these timeless words: "And the Lord did according to the word of Moses." The frogs started dying all over the country. The people piled the dead frogs up in heaps, and the country stank. But then, Pharaoh conveniently forgot his promise to let the people go once the frogs had been exterminated.

On the path of spiritual education, one must always remember that the Lord will stretch us until the thread is so thin, it disappears under who He is. To illustrate that point, we see God bringing ten plagues upon the nation, instead of just two or three.

Once again, the Lord brought Moses to His side and instructed him to tell Aaron how to bring lice upon the land. The lice came up from the dust of the earth and were all over the people and their animals throughout Egypt. Then the magicians came again for the next round of this new game, "Moses against the Magicians."

> And the magicians did so with their enchantments to bring forth lice, but they could not: so there were lice upon man and upon beast. Then the magicians said unto Pharaoh, This is the finger of God: and Pharaoh's heart was hardened, and he hearkened not unto them; as the Lord had said (Exodus 8:18–19).

I bet the Egyptians were relieved at this point that the magicians couldn't do anything more. How much lice can one person stand, anyway?

Isn't it interesting that the magicians could never undo what God was doing—nobody can! They can only add insult to injury and make the situation worse. But they cannot touch what God has marked. The magicians recognized that this was God, the I AM, the one who far exceeded who they were. They took note that these things were happening because of a mere "finger of God," and decided they'd had enough. We have His whole heart and hand upon us; how much greater will those miracles be for us when they come! God's just moving the frogs and lice out of the way and purifying the water that flows around us.

No Room for Insecurity or Arrogance

There is no room for insecurity or arrogance with the rod of God in our hand. Moses must have known, without a doubt, that he could do it. On our own, mistakes will abound, but in Christ, surely we can do all things because He will strengthen us. When our hearts are open before God and we have laid everything down before Him, then it's easy because we have nothing left to hide. Our hidden emotions are already known to God; they just get in the way of us truly knowing God, walking with Him, and allowing Him to move through us.

All this time, through the blood, the frogs and the lice, God was manifesting His signs and wonders, power and miracles through Aaron. Moses was the silent partner up until then. He had been a willing vessel, but an insecure one, up to this point. Moses would learn who this God was as he danced with Him in the moonlight of miracles.

Are you willing to dance the dance of miracles with the Lord? Moses was taking dance lessons at this point. Lessons teach you how to stay off the other person's feet and how to keep time with the music. But if you never show up for practice, you won't be any good at it and you will ruin the beauty of the dance. Start showing up to learn the dance, and you'll see how amazing it can be. You show up by stopping your need to control everything and letting God be God. Yes, even in the middle of your mess! Often these things are a calculated decision, and nothing more. Once you have prayed for help, the Lord rushes in; but then there you are, needing to choose how to behave in the middle of it.

Maybe you have been the reluctant vessel: willing but unable. It is the willing heart into which God will pour His ability. It is in the unable vessel that God's glory can be truly seen and known.

Should I try and persevere to accomplish things? Yes! Should I attempt to follow a dream bigger than I am? Yes! Should I make efforts toward education and experience, training and learning? Yes! But when all is said and done, as the book of Romans shouts at us, it's great that you have prepared to run the race, but it is only God who gives the mercy for the running of the race! *God's grace enables us to rise up and do what Christ is calling us to do, while His mercy allows us the opportunity to accomplish it.*

Whether you have all the ability in the world or none of it, lay down those securities and insecurities. Then you will be gloriously unable and allow God room to be able.

CHAPTER 15

Developing Trust and Obedience

And the Lord said unto Moses, Rise up early in the morning, and stand before Pharaoh; lo, he cometh forth to the water; and say unto him, Thus saith the Lord, Let my people go, that they may serve me. Else, if thou wilt not let my people go, behold, I will send swarms of flies upon thee, and upon thy servants, and upon thy people, and into thy houses: and the houses of the Egyptians shall be full of swarms of flies, and also the ground whereon they are. And I will sever in that day the land of Goshen, in which my people dwell, that no swarms of flies shall be there; to the end thou mayest know that I am the Lord in the midst of the earth. And I will put a division between my people and thy people: tomorrow shall this sign be. And the Lord did so; and there came a grievous swarm of flies into the house of Pharaoh, and into his servants' houses, and into all the land of Egypt: the land was corrupted by reason of the swarm of flies (Exodus 8:20–24).

The land is "corrupted" because of a swarm of flies. Not just flies, but a "swarm of flies"! I don't think I've ever seen a swarm of flies. If I were to see a swarm of flies today, I don't think I'd see them just picking on everyone on one side of the street! It would appear that God was using everything in existence to separate these people—provoking one to be free and the other to set them free.

God is very clear about something here: My people and your people are two different people! There was a mixed multitude that emerged from Egypt. They would have to be shown the Father so He could be known by them. The plagues made this people able to see God as He is. They would follow Moses out of Egypt in an attempt to know this God who called them, and they would do it because they saw triumph overcome trial. God brought blood, frogs and lice through Aaron, and now God would simply "show up" while Moses spoke His words for the next couple of plagues. One of the greatest ways to learn how to trust God is to simply sit back and watch who He is. Moses wouldn't have to give instruction to lead a nation—not yet. He wouldn't have to stare Pharaoh down—not yet. He wouldn't have to hold his arms out in obedience all night long—not yet. For now, Moses just had to speak what God told him to say. God is long-suffering with our learning and doesn't put on us more than we can bear. When it was time for Moses to be launched as God's secret weapon, he would be fully armed, having lost himself to who God is.

Can't you just see God drawing close to Moses and calling him to come closer through each trial? "Trust me a little more," the Lord was saying, "just a little closer—that's it. Just a few more trials and you will know who I am. I am going to remove all that stands between us so you can see Me more clearly."

The flies God sent as a plague were not just a few houseflies; they were a "grievous swarm of flies." They covered Egypt, but not the land of Goshen, where the Israelites lived. The Lord protected His people from the wrath that surrounded them. God then told Moses to meet with Pharaoh. He didn't tell him to tell Aaron anything this time—He told Moses to get the job done himself. So Moses talked to Pharaoh, and true to form, God arrived in style! At this point, I'm not sure why Moses wasn't being told to use the rod; it seemed to be the "weapon of choice" in the past. I suppose God wanted nothing between Him and Moses right now. There would be time for a rod and a stick later. There would be time for lots of things later, but at this point God wanted Moses to Himself, with Moses leaning on nothing and no one else but God.

Operating as a Vessel of God

When you declare before a burning bush that you are willing to be the vessel of God, you must allow God to reveal Himself through that willingness before the throne of Pharaoh. It's not always easy, and often you will be misunderstood, but you must submit to the One you have yielded your life to, so that He will be seen and not you.

Once again, Pharaoh said that he would let the people go; the flies were just too much for him. And, once again, Moses asked God to remove the flies, and God did. It is no small mystery that, after the flies were gone, Pharaoh changed his mind and wouldn't let the people go.

Moses had been busy responding to the cry of Pharaoh's heart, not God's. He hadn't yet understood that God was actually the One he was taking his orders from. To operate as a vessel of God, we each must understand the value of being held up by the Spirit and not held down by the flesh.

Being a vessel of God is to prove God among mankind. Pharaoh was watching. The Egyptian nation was watching, and all of Israel was watching. They were all watching Moses, wondering how he would respond to God and what God would do next. They were judging the faithfulness of God based upon Moses. The world watched Moses, just as they are watching us.

God didn't operate through Moses to bring the flies or the death to the cattle that came next; Moses wasn't ready to handle that yet. He was still allowing his manhood to shout louder than his God; and a vessel of God must only hear one voice—God's! In His great mercy, God asked Moses to merely speak, and He would perform— no rod, no drama, just speak. The very thing Moses said earlier he was not able to do, God was proving to him that, in His power, he could do. He no longer had a speech problem, because Pharaoh was hearing him just fine, and so was God.

Please notice that the magicians weren't anywhere to be found when God sent the flies or the death to the cattle. They might be able to play "pick up sticks" with a man struggling to be a vessel, but they couldn't play that game with God, so they were noticeably absent!

> Then the Lord said unto Moses, Go in unto Pharaoh, and tell him, Thus saith the Lord God of the Hebrews, Let my people go, that they may serve me. For if thou refuse to let them go, and wilt hold them still, Behold, the hand of the Lord is upon thy cattle which is in the field, upon the horses, upon the asses, upon the camels, upon the oxen, and upon the sheep: there shall be a very grievous murrain. And the Lord shall sever between the cattle of Israel and the cattle of Egypt: and there shall nothing die of all that is the children's of Israel. And the Lord appointed a set time, saying, Tomorrow the Lord shall do this thing in the land. And the Lord did that thing on the morrow, and all the cattle of Egypt died: but of the cattle of the children of Israel died not one (Exodus 9:1–6).

So, once again, the Lord produced the plague by His own hand: "And the Lord did that thing." He was showing Moses who He was. Moses was still afraid to really let God be who He was in him. Not Moses in God, but God in Moses. This dynamic hadn't happened yet, but it would. The plagues were serving some great purposes. The Egyptians were seeing the hand of the mighty God that the Israelites had been talking about for centuries, and Moses was standing there with them, taking it all in. He was coming to the revelation that would be the foundation of friendship: He was not the deliverer, but God was! We can do nothing without Him, and when we try, we are left with dead bodies at our feet that need to be explained away. He was now getting a glimpse of the God he left Egypt 40 years ago to pursue. Moses was moving slowly toward Him, but at least he was moving. He was beginning to believe God could do it, but would He do it for him?

That's the age-old question, isn't it? I believe God heals, but will He do it for me? I believe God brings people together supernaturally, but will He bring me a spouse? God is a God of abundance, but I'm not sure He will bring me out of poverty. These are the questions that can forbid us from moving in the freedom of trusting God.

A Good Answer

Becoming a vessel of God means learning to trust Him fully. Part of that "becoming" is a willingness to demonstrate Christ to others through our obedience to, and steadfast assurance in, Christ. Moses had to be willing to show Pharaoh how to obey.

When Pharaoh asks, "Who is God and why do you believe in Him?" we have to have a good answer, a right answer. We live the answer with our lives, more than our words. Moses had to be willing to believe God, even if he didn't understand Him.

> *Moses had to be willing to believe God,*
> *even if he didn't understand Him.*

So now we have dead cattle. The Egyptians' cattle were all dead, and as a testimony to the power of God, the Israelites' cattle were alive and well. God wanted to be sure it was understood that this plague was no mistake, and that He did it on purpose. Pharaoh was mad again, so mad that he didn't even offer to deceive Moses this time. He just flatly stated that he would not let the people go!

Moses was closer to becoming a vessel of God now, than ever before. Seeing all those dead cows on one side of the street and the living ones on the other had given him courage; and so he launched out into the deep with his God. You don't hear any excuses now. You don't hear Moses telling God about how he can't and how they won't anymore, you simply hear the sound of his sandals crushing sand beneath him as he moved toward God.

> *And the Lord said unto Moses and unto Aaron, Take to*
> *you handfuls of ashes of the furnace, and let Moses sprin-*
> *kle it toward the heaven in the sight of Pharaoh. And it*

> *shall become small dust in all the land of Egypt, and shall*
> *be a boil breaking forth with blains upon man, and upon*
> *beast, throughout all the land of Egypt. And they took*
> *ashes of the furnace, and stood before Pharaoh; and Mo-*
> *ses sprinkled it up toward heaven; and it became a boil*
> *breaking forth with blains upon man, and upon beast.*
> *And the magicians could not stand before Moses because*
> *of the boils; for the boil was upon the magicians, and upon*
> *all the Egyptians* (Exodus 9:8–11).

Look at what happened at this point: God was no longer instructing Aaron. He bypassed Aaron and reached out to Moses with the opportunity of the ages, and Moses took it. "And Moses sprinkled it [the ashes] up toward heaven." The boils that came were so fantastic and furious that they covered all the people and the animals. Moses was actively taking part in the wonders of God and allowing God to move through him. He was no longer just telling Aaron what to do and shivering in the shadows. He was a man of God, attempting to become a vessel of God. You get the feeling that he was still a little nervous, because Aaron still stood next to him, showing him how to get it done as God instructed him. But very shortly, he would learn to handle it. You cannot walk this road as a rejected child, but only as an accepted heir!

Then the declaration of freedom from emotional torment was made: "And the magicians could not stand before Moses because of the boils; for the boil was upon the magicians, and upon all the Egyptians." They have finally seen God in Moses, and He looked powerful!

The reason Moses could obey at this point is because he had gained a trust for this God he had chosen to serve. We have observed the evolution of a vessel of God, a man who was about to leave his old self behind!

Evidently Moses had a horrible fear of the magicians. His insecurity was so great that it caused him to question the power of God. It wasn't until after the magicians left for good that Moses rose to the occasion. Moses had feared the magicians, battled them and overcame them, until they were no more. The magicians represented an insecurity in Moses, a lack of confidence in his God; but once they were gone, he was able to see God more clearly and trust Him. As he fought his own issues of rejection and all the manifestations of it, he became whole and well. It is only then that he was able to fight the evil that surrounded him and trust God to do what He said He would do in the middle of it. This is the desire of God for us all: to battle and overcome until the insecurities and fears of our own hearts are no more.

It happened that way for Isaiah, too. In Isaiah 6, it wasn't until King Uzziah was dead that Isaiah "saw the Lord high and lifted up." Job experienced the same thing when he began to "see" God rather than only "hear" Him. David said, "It is good that I have been afflicted, for now I see you clearly."

When everything else is out of the way, our vision is restored. When we lay our kings down, our positions down, our opinions down, our comforts down, then we shall see Christ clearly.

Honesty

When the source of our insecurity is dealt with, then we can come to God with an honesty that won't be held hostage to our old wounds. There is nothing left to defend but the truth, so our wounds can't shout for protection when our fear has been dealt with!

Moses had gone from being a mere man to being a man of God and, finally, to being a vessel of God. He began to trust this God whose hand he had fallen into. The man was no longer in the way; for the desire to be a vessel had arrived!

As far as I can tell, everything we've seen until now has been a "warm up" to the main event. God told Moses to inform Pharaoh that if he didn't let the people go...well, listen for yourself: "For I will at this time send all my plagues upon thine heart, and upon thy servants, and upon thy people; that thou mayest know that there is none like me in all the earth. For now I will stretch out my hand, that I may smite thee and thy people with pestilence; and thou shalt be cut off from the earth" (Exodus 9:14-15).

God then told them that He was also going to send hail upon the earth, such as the earth had never seen before. God warned them that they had better get everybody inside, including the animals, because it was coming.

This hail was going to be so bad that it was going to wipe out everything in its path: plants, people, and animals. And, there was our man Moses, no longer only a man from Midian, but a man from Midian who had chosen to be the vessel of God. He now moved to a different tune. He was not afraid to take ownership of what God was doing in him. Only when we are willing to take the risk of ownership can we offer it back to God. We can only offer to Him what we own.

David knew this truth when he purchased Ornan, the Jebusite's field, in which to offer a sacrifice to God. Isaiah knew it when he warned those with unclean hands not to touch the holy things. Nehemiah knew it when he allowed his life to declare that ownership meant putting forth effort at the wall. Jesus Christ knew it the day He owned Calvary.

Earlier, I think Moses figured that as long as he was far enough away from what God was doing, he couldn't get blamed if anything went wrong. At this point, Moses, hidden in the arms of God, wasn't tormented by the words of men any longer. He was inspired and comforted by the words of God. He didn't care what Pharaoh or the magicians said anymore, and he didn't doubt his calling, not even if the people he was leading did. He only cared what God thought. You are about to see a man "go for broke"!

> *And Moses stretched forth his rod toward heaven: and the Lord sent thunder and hail, and the fire ran along upon the ground; and the Lord rained hail upon the land of Egypt. So there was hail, and fire mingled with the hail, very grievous, such as there was none like it in all the land of Egypt since it became a nation. And the hail smote throughout all the land of Egypt all that was in the field, both man and beast; and the hail smote every herb of the field, and brake every tree of the field. Only in the land of Goshen where the children of Israel were, was there no hail (Exodus 9:23–26).*

This story leaves us with hail big enough to break trees and fire spewing down from heaven. Okay, I guess God's done! There must have been thunder along with it, because Pharaoh finally asked for the "mighty thunderings" to stop. Earlier, some of Pharaoh's servants were afraid of "the word of the Lord," and so they put their cattle inside and hid before the hail hit, at the warning of Moses. Pharaoh finally said that he and his servants had sinned against God, and they recognized that God was the one righteous God. Pharaoh even called himself and his people "wicked."

Pharaoh begged for mercy, as he had always done with Moses. The hail busting up trees around him and uncontrollable fire dancing on his head were just too much. He had signs and wonders all around him that were shouting, "God is out of man's control!" Pharaoh was somebody who God knew would not give in easily. Time after time, when he relented and repented, he did it in form only. Of course, when the snakes aren't hissing at your ankles anymore, the promises you made are easily forgotten. Somewhere, Pharaoh had learned the system, and what had worked for him yesterday among a people he controlled wasn't working today, when those people were sold-out to walking with God. *When you allow God to be in control of your life, Pharaoh can't control you anymore.*

Pharaoh was always able to manipulate Moses into getting from God what he wanted. Pharaoh was always able to lean upon the fear and wound hidden deep within the soul of Moses to get what he wanted from God. Pharaoh was always able to convince Moses that his need was more important than God's desires. This is something a vessel of God must never allow. Mere men allow it; a true vessel of honor won't!

Moses wasn't falling for it this time. When Pharaoh began to cry and whine and declare his false repentance before Moses, Pharaoh must have been surprised at his response. Pharaoh said, "Entreat the Lord for me," but the man on the other end wasn't stuttering! He wasn't going to start begging God for Pharaoh again. He was no longer struggling with who God was in him. Moses wasn't Pharaoh's puppet anymore because of his own fear; instead, he had become the vessel of God, a mouthpiece worth listening to. The next time Pharaoh called for the man from Midian, he found Moses, the vessel of God, unwilling to lean on Aaron any longer, for he had learned to lean on God!

The most amazing thing happened next. We have a picture of Moses not begging God or entreating Him on behalf of Pharaoh, as he did so many times before as a mere man. Now we have this vessel of God knowing who he is, who God is, and what the Lord has told him to do, and refusing to waver from that. Moses no longer needed to beg God to deliver the situation; instead, he rose up in the middle of the situation and handled it, showing others how to trust and obey.

Pharaoh had told Moses he repented and his people repented. He acknowledged God as the righteous Lord and begged Moses to help him. Then Pharaoh went on to say that he not only wanted Moses to leave with the people, but he wouldn't allow them to stay. That was the best lunch conversation they'd had yet. If there would be any time to be moved, it would be now. But Moses was immovable, for his heart had learned to trust the Lord. "Thou will keep him in perfect peace whose mind is stayed on thee, because he trusts in thee. Trust ye in the Lord forever, for in the Lord Jehovah is everlasting strength" (Isaiah 26:3–4).

Moses was now a man on fire, not wondering anymore what God would do or not do, for he knew! Listen to him as he makes a declaration that only trust can produce:

> *And Moses said unto him, As soon as I am gone out of the city, I will spread abroad my hands unto the Lord; and the thunder shall cease, neither shall there be any more hail; that thou mayest know how that the earth is the Lord's. But as for thee and thy servants, I know that ye will not yet fear the Lord God (Exodus 9:29–30).*

Moses left the city and stretched out his arms as he said he would and didn't even check with God to see if it was right, because he knew it was right. He was walking in unity with his God because he had walked past his fears, rejections and wounds. He no longer wondered—he knew. All that he had declared before Pharaoh happened. Moses was finally on the same page as the Lord. He even told Pharaoh what the Lord had been telling him all along:

"Pharaoh won't fear Me, and I'm going to have to harden his heart." Moses had fought the wisdom of it before, but now he had become part of the process. He had gone from not believing to believing, and now was walking in a level of trust that said, "All I need is the Word, and I will respond to it."

CHAPTER 16

Weapon of Choice

Going forward from this point, I cannot imagine the chaos that would have taken place if Moses was still arguing with God. To be a vessel of God, you must decide that you have already lost the argument. That's the only thing that takes the power of your opinion away. Moses was qualified to carry the promises because he was not carrying anything else. Moses had now become God's weapon of choice—a vessel of honor. He would no longer give Aaron instruction in Egypt.

> *How long wilt thou refuse to humble thyself before me? Let my people go that they may serve me. Else, if thou refuse to let my people go, behold, to morrow will I bring the locusts into thy coast: And they shall cover the face of the earth, that one cannot be able to see the earth; and they shall eat the residue of that which is escaped, which remaineth unto you from the hail, and shall eat every tree which groweth for you out of the field. And, they shall fill thy houses and the houses of all thy servants and the houses of all the Egyptians; which neither thy fathers, nor thy fathers' fathers have seen, since the day that they were upon the earth unto this day. And Moses turned himself and went out from Pharaoh (Exodus 10:3–6).*

Now, that is quite a speech! I don't see any shaking or stuttering going on here. You get the picture of a man in charge: a man who knows what God told him to do; a vessel of God not operating out of wounds, but out of power—God's power! What a sight that must have been—Moses fully charged before the man who ruled the world but was destined to lose it. I picture Moses no longer cowering, leaning on Aaron, timid about picking up the rod, worried about snakes, watching and wondering, hiding or making excuses. He was simply standing with his God before the heathen king, shouting, "Let the people go—and do it now!" What a joy it has been to watch this man become a vessel.

Confidence is different than arrogance. Assurance is different than pride. To be separated is different than independence, and single-mindedness is different than rebellion. The new confidence that Moses possessed at this point came from his fellowship with God.

Of course, Pharaoh was always up for a challenge, so the locusts came, and they came with force. God created a mighty east wind, and it blew for a whole day and continued to blow through the night. In the morning, it blew in the locusts! As the Lord said, they covered the whole earth:

> *For they covered the face of the whole earth, so that the land was darkened; and they did eat every herb of the land, and all the fruit of the trees which the hail had left: and there remained not any green thing in the trees, or in the herbs of the field, through all the land of Egypt* (Exodus 10:15).

It's as if the Lord was deliberately being merciful to these people who would not listen. He commanded the hail to leave some leaves on the trees and some herbs and fruit. But the people would never get to enjoy them because their disobedience would soon manifest in the forms of darkness and locusts to destroy the provision. Imagine enough locusts to "cover the face of the whole earth, so that the land was darkened." The sound of the locusts eating the last bit of food you had left and the horror of not being able to stop them or see them because of the darkness they created would be almost unbearable. But Pharaoh would still insist on being Pharaoh.

Being manipulated by man and being moved by God are two entirely different things.

True to form, Pharaoh then called for Moses and Aaron and admitted his sin once again. But Moses was unmoved. Then Pharaoh asked for forgiveness, and that was something different. He was saying, "I haven't asked for forgiveness before and I may not ask for it again, but I'm asking now." He had a moment of sincere repentance. So Moses responded, but not as before. Earlier, when Moses "entreated God" for Pharaoh, he begged God out of his own insecurities and fears. To "entreat," as Moses used it earlier, holds the nuance of begging. He begged God much of the time before because he was afraid of Pharaoh. But now, when he entreated God, he was actually interceding for Pharaoh. "Entreat" (*athar*, #H6279) literally means to "intercede." Mere men can't "entreat" like that— only vessels can! While men beg, vessels intercede. Being manipulated by man and being moved by God are two entirely different things. Vessels of God don't need the approval of man because they are walking in God's approval.

The Cause of Darkness

The Lord responded by sending a mighty west wind to drive the locusts out into the Red Sea. The locusts were finally gone; not one was left on the coasts of Egypt. And almost immediately, God told Moses to stretch out his hand toward heaven. Moses obeyed. A darkness fell upon the whole earth. This wasn't just any darkness, either. It was a thick darkness that could be "felt," and it remained for three days. People couldn't see one another, and basically nobody moved. But as a testimony to God's abounding favor and response to His desire to receive honor in all things, every Israelite house had light in it! Just imagine the thrill of three days and nights spent in the Israelite camp during this time. God's inspired, beautiful light filled their houses, while "on the other side of the tracks," everyone else was groping around in the dark, not able to see anything. Worse than that, it was a darkness that was creepy and heavy, and you could actually *feel the darkness.* God brought the light to honor Himself as well as provide for His people.

When a thick darkness comes, it is usually there to introduce death of some kind. When the darkness comes in our lives, it's time to look at it and discover its cause. We often ignore the darkness because it represents a battle that we don't want to face. If we crave comfort and are continually looking for ways to live in peace, shrouded by misplaced mercy (which is actually a lulling, seducing spirit), then we will discount the darkness as nothing and cry that it doesn't exist. But no matter how comfortable our bed is, if we never get out of it, we will still get bedsores! We will simply label "the darkness that can be felt" as fog and convince ourselves that the sun has just set early that day. Peace, comfort and mercy are good, but not at the expense of purity, holiness and truth! The first step to walking in sin is to justify compromise, and the second step is to defend it. Moses is done forsaking the power of God for the purposes of men.

Pharaoh now wanted the people gone, but only if they left their animals. Bad decision! Pharaoh got mad at Moses and, once again, refused to let them go. Pharaoh wanted to obey his way, and God wanted the obedience to come His way!

Pharaoh told Moses to leave and threatened that, if he ever saw him again, Moses would die. At that point, Moses pretty much said, "Fine with me—see ya!" He was an unbothered, abundant vessel of God. His biggest concern now was hearing God, not the people and not Pharaoh.

In chapter 11 God told Moses what was going to happen. The Israelites were told to borrow gold and silver from their Egyptian neighbors. The Lord gave them favor in the sight of the Egyptians, who started giving them all kinds of stuff. Moses was now considered a great man by both the Egyptians and their slaves. As a man, Moses might have been moved by the praises the people gave him; but as a vessel, he was greatly unimpressed by it! The Lord let Moses know that the last plague was upon them, and they should get ready to walk into the promise. All the firstborn would die in the Egyptian households. Even the firstborn of their animals would die.

By then, the plagues had outlived their usefulness because Moses had successfully arrived in the land where vessels live, and God had received glory for all the deliverance He had brought through the plagues.

Sometimes while we are waiting to be delivered from our own plagues, we can lose sight of the promises. Waiting is the great holding area for the emotions that fight trust. The concerns of "I" rise up to destroy trust: "What if I look bad?" "What if I am not taken care of?" "What if I get hurt?" or, the most famous one, "What if I didn't hear God after all?" Sarah lost sight of her promise when she convinced Abraham to go with Hagar. King Saul did the same thing when he performed the sacrifice without Samuel. Jehu did when he put himself in the equation of deliverance. Peter did when he denied the Lord. Many of us have, from time to time; it's a dangerous place to visit, and there is no guarantee of our ever leaving. In the great land of waiting, if we keep focused on the Lord's desires and are not consumed with our own needs, then we will be successful and able to move on to the new beginnings He has designed for us.

A New Beginning
Exodus 12 declares a new beginning for the people. The Lord instituted the Passover supper. He told them what to cook and how to cook it; when to eat it and how to eat it. He instructed them to be ready to leave when He told them to. He wanted them in their running shoes, and told them to eat in a hurry because He was coming! That's how the promises are sometimes. It seems like we are in plagues forever and ever. And then, suddenly, that's it! The game is over, and the Lord comes with His promise.

The Lord told the Israelites to brush the doorposts of their homes with the blood of lambs and stay inside until morning and not to come out. They were told to use hyssop branches to apply this blood. (It is the hyssop branch that was used to offer Jesus vinegar to drink while He was on Calvary's cross. God knew from the beginning of time even what branch of which bush would need redemption. He knows about the hyssop branch; surely He knows about you!)

> *And the blood shall be to you for a token upon the houses where ye are: and when I see the blood, I will pass over you, and the plague shall not be upon you to destroy you, when I smite the land of Egypt* (Exodus 12:13).

It's still true today: "When I see the blood, I will pass over you!" He's passing by this way—are you ready to receive His blessings as He pushes the plagues away from you? Men and women are never properly prepared to receive from God, but vessels are. Men and women can imagine that their greatness brought the promise. Men and women can be paralyzed in fear and handicap their gifts. Men and women can strike out in insecurity because of rejection. But vessels only respond to God because they have crucified their flesh with Christ.

God didn't need the blood on the doorpost because He had bad vision or no discernment to know which children were His. He wanted it there so that the people could participate in the promise through obedience. Abundance will always be waiting for you on the other side of your obedience. God lets us in on the plan so that we can pray and then get out of the way! People often want to know how to hear God. Here's the secret: Pray-Peace-Pursue. If we have one, we get the other. If we have no peace, then we should not pursue it!

To hear God effectively we have to trust Him. Otherwise, our heart will be so busy protecting itself that it can't truly hear truth. It takes a discipline of flesh to be still enough to find out what the Lord is saying, and then be brave and trusting enough to pray for it to come to pass, no matter what the cost.

> *And it came to pass, that at midnight the Lord smote all the firstborn in the land of Egypt, from the firstborn of Pharaoh that sat on his throne unto the firstborn of the captive that was in the dungeon; and all the firstborn of cattle. And Pharaoh rose up in the night, he, and all his servants, and all the Egyptians; and there was a great cry*

in Egypt; for there was not a house where there was not one dead. And he called for Moses and Aaron by night, and said, Rise up, and get you forth from among my people, both ye and the children of Israel; and go, serve the Lord, as ye have said. Also take your flocks and your herds, as ye have said, and be gone; and bless me also. And the Egyptians were urgent upon the people, that they might send them out of the land in haste; for they said, we be all dead men (Exodus 12:29–33).

Pharaoh had had it; in fact, the whole country had had it. They wanted the people of God gone, and would consider it a great blessing if they just left! In a tragic slam as a result of willful disobedience and rebellion of the king, all the firstborn of Egypt had died. The firstborn human, the firstborn beast, probably even the firstborn rat and fly and plant. Firstborn everything—gone!

The Egyptians wanted the Israelites gone so badly that they gave them their valuables while they were shoving them out the door. The Bible says that the Israelites actually "spoiled" the Egyptians. To "spoil" means to take all the plunder of war. In other words, in a battle, whoever won got to take away whatever they could carry from the defeated army or country. It was a rite of victory in battle that the winners got to enjoy. So, it had truly been a battle that the Lord had been fighting for them, and He won! The Israelites left Egypt with all the spoils of war, heading toward the promised land, for the plagues were over. We are told that there were 600,000 men who left—and that's not including the women and children. That's a lot of people to care for, but God was committed to that course. Some guess that there were anywhere from four to 12 million Israelites who made the exodus. And God provided abundantly for each and every one! They would get food from heaven, water from rocks; and even their shoes would never wear out.

The Bonus
While preaching in the Midwest a couple of years ago, I ran into a woman who I call the "bonus lady." At a meeting, I asked if there

was anyone with a testimony they wanted to share. And, from way in the back of the convention center, this woman shouted out, "Yes, I do!" She was given a microphone and proceeded to tell us that earlier in the service, God had supernaturally healed her arthritic leg and broken foot. She was jumping all around and shouting praises to God. She said that she didn't care if she lost her eyesight, just as long as her foot and leg were well. This lady was just so thrilled to be able to walk again. She said, "I know that sometimes when God heals us of something, He allows illness to manifest in another area."

"What?" I said, confused. "Bring her up here."

I couldn't see her very well because of the size of the convention center, but the closer she got, the more comical I realized the situation was. She was saying how it was okay because she was willing to pay for her healed leg and foot with her eyes. I just kept quiet, knowing that Jesus had already paid for her sickness.

She got closer to the stage, and I came down to where she was. Then I asked her to remove her eyeglasses. Evidently, the old prescription was messing up her now perfect vision! She began to shout and scream, saying, "Oh, I got a bonus! I got a bonus!" I explained that God is the God of bonuses and doesn't want her paying for her healing with other pain. A few days later, she was back at the meeting and announced that the doctor said she now had 20/20 vision.

Sent out with Grace and Provision

God isn't just going to send you out. He is going to send you out with grace and provision, with more than you bargained for!

Sometimes while you are waiting to leave your Egypt, it can appear that you are entertaining eternity. But God cannot lie to you. What He has told you in the Word and deposited in your heart will come to pass—just keep walking with Him. Just keep showing up. He'll make it all happen, and if you are weary of the battle, simply stop and let Him take it.

There was a mixed multitude going with the people of flocks, herds and cattle, along with all their baking ovens and cooking gear. Their food had been quickly thrown together for the trip, and they gathered together in their tribes, or "armies," and headed to Succoth. It had taken 430 years to arrive at the place where they were stepping out of Egypt as a free people. They would soon discover that freedom itself must sometimes be conquered.

"And it came to pass the selfsame day, that the Lord did bring the children of Israel out of the land of Egypt by their armies" (Exodus 12:51).

So, now they are leaving Egypt: the exodus begins! Yet, it would appear later on, as they looked back on this moment, that their troubles had not ended, but just begun. Right when God sets us up for the biggest miracle, sometimes all we can do is concentrate on the problems around us. We can forget that God's solutions are always bigger than our problems. If you have a big problem, then you must need a big miracle, and God is big enough to do it. When you can't have finance, He will give you favor. When you can't have healing, He will give you peace. When you can't have a relationship with someone else, He will give you fellowship with Him. Stop looking at what you can't, don't and won't have, and start looking at the glorious attributes that you do have simply because you are a child of God. It is never about the destination, but always about the journey. When your journey is difficult, it's easy to want it to be over. But remember, the journey will prove you and keep you. The journey is where the miracles abound, if you let them.

CHAPTER 17

Betty Lou

I learned how to expect a miracle and catch a vision from my father, but I learned how to persevere until it got here from my mother, Betty Lou. Years ago, I asked her to write me a story that would tell a piece of her life. I asked her if she'd rather I tell this story after she was having dinner with Jesus, and she said very firmly, "No, I'm not ashamed of anything, because it's all under the blood of Jesus. If my life can bless somebody, then that makes it all the more worthwhile to me and glorifying to Jesus; because, but for the grace of God, there go I." Thanks, Ma—your transparency has always made it easy to see Jesus right through you.

Hers is an overcoming story, and she has only shared a small portion of it; and even with that, I have left segments of it out. But in light of what we have just seen Moses do, I thought you'd enjoy watching somebody else leave their flesh behind.

My mother has written this in her own hand and entitled it,

Do You Trust God or Not?
First of all, this is not a sad, "poor me" story. It's just a few things that I have encountered on this journey of life. Things that have caused me to ask the question, "Do I trust God or not?" At first I didn't ask myself this question. I didn't know there was such a question.

It's somewhat of a miracle that I was even born. In 1931, my father was a 17-year-old "motorcycle dude," and my mother was a

15-year-old "motorcycle mama." I was an unwanted "thing," and my mom tried to get rid of me in many ways before I was ever born. She says she jumped off tall tables and chairs, and took hot sulfur baths. The long willow branch should have really hurt (ouch), but God had another plan for me, because nothing she did could hurt me—I survived! When the time came for me to be born, they drove up on the Harley motorcycle to my grandma's house and hatched me with Grandma's help, stayed a few hours, and then left. I didn't see my parents again for seven years.

One day my father called and told my grandmother to get me ready, because he was taking me home to take care of their two other kids and the house, because my mother was having a mental breakdown. My brother, whom I never met, had died at seven months old. So, I went home to be the maid and caregiver to my two younger sisters while my father went to work.

I knew that I was not loved, and at an early age, I knew my purpose was to be used. Thinking back on it, I guess it seemed okay at the time; there was nothing that I could do, so I tried to not be a problem. When I left Grandma's house she said to me, "Be a good girl, and I love you!" Somehow, that was enough.

One day about three years later, I was coming home from the grocery store and I heard music coming from a building that used to be a store. I was about ten years old, with straight, stringy white hair. I had warts all over my hands, and I didn't have any friends. People called me "warthog." I did the best I could, but I didn't really have anyone to teach me how to care for myself. My main job was to be sure that my brothers and sisters were taken care of, and I tried my best to help them and make sure they did their homework so they could do something good someday. They hated me for that, but it was my job, so I kept at it no matter what they did to me. I never had a friend and didn't really know what that was. The music in this building sounded so nice, so I went in, sat down and listened.

Someone was playing the piano; another was playing the drums; another, a trumpet; and another had the tambourine. All the people up front were wearing uniforms. When the music stopped, a man in a uniform got up and started talking about this real good friend he had. This friend was always there for him to talk with, cry with and to have fun with. Then he said, "If anyone wants to meet my friend, just come on up here!" He said to come up and he would tell them about his friend. Well, hey! This was gonna be great! I didn't have any friends, so I went up.

I guess you know by now the people in the uniforms were the Salvation Army, and the friend was Jesus! The man told me Jesus would be my friend and love me like nobody else ever could. He told me that Jesus loved me so much that He would be my friend forever and love me always. The man told me that Jesus would never, ever leave me once I asked Him to come and live in my heart. He put his hands on my head and prayed that Jesus would come into my life. He asked Jesus to lead, guide and direct me. Then he asked Jesus to protect me. Well, that was that, I thought. But none of my people were Christians, and the only "Jesus" they knew was a swear word; but God had a plan, anyway.

The very next day one of my older cousins came to live with us. Almost from the first night he was there, he started molesting me. I was ten years old at the time. I hid in different places so maybe he couldn't find me, but he always did. He said if I told, he would kill my younger sisters. He showed me his gun, and I believed him because he was mean enough to do it. He told me that he would know if I told anyone. Every day, for as long as I can remember during those years, he was always there, every single day....

Finally, after three years, I took a chance and secretly called my grandma. I told her what was going on, and she came to get me from San Francisco, where we were living. There was a big fight, and my cousin disappeared, and I went home with Grandma. I was about 13 years old when this happened. I was very afraid of men. If people even breathed deeply around me, I had a reaction to it. I couldn't pass by a man without shaking all over. I tried to find Jesus during those years, but I couldn't. I knew that He must be in my heart like the Salvation Army man said, but I couldn't find Him. But still, God had a plan.

I realize now that God chose me to be the one to stand for Him in my family. He knew that because of circumstances, I would be strong enough to be called names, be friendless and not be able to trust anyone but Him. Grandma instilled right and wrong in me, and I didn't want to disappoint her.

So much for that, because just about this time, my father called again and said he was coming to get me to take care of the other kids again. So, at 14, I was the "mother" to four other children. My mother was gone most of the time with other men. And my dad was always gone working or at the bars. Without any Christian friends, church or knowing about the Bible, I soon forgot about Jesus.

There was this girl across the street who was 17 years old and she really liked me. She was always so nice to me and thoughtful. She introduced me to the lesbian lifestyle. Every minute I could be with her was proof that someone besides Grandma loved me. We gave each other what we "needed." This went on for two years, then I went back home to Grandma's house to take care of her. I came to know the lesbian lifestyle was wrong and unpleasing to the Lord during my time at Grandma's, and I forsook it. I was trying to go to high school during this time, but I was so far behind it seemed like an impossible task. I was working hard to get caught up, and it seemed like I was going to reach my goals when, you guessed it, six months before graduation, I went back home to take care of the kids again. Somehow, I got through school, went to work and got married. For me, this was the beginning of the question, "Do you trust God or not?" Praise His name!

My husband's family were Christians, and we came from "different sides of the tracks." My mother-in-law didn't like me very much. I was considered "bad." But I loved her and was determined to show her that there was good in me. Before the end of her life, we would be closer than a mother and a daughter. She was the only mother I ever knew, and she learned to love me as Jesus did, with all her heart!

When my first child was born, she didn't do well. Her name was Cynthia. I didn't know where Jesus was at that time, but I talked to God a lot. I wanted my baby to live. But after four days, I told God, "If You want her, You can have her." And He did.

About eight years later, my daughter, Gail, was three years old when she drank some gasoline by accident. We rushed her to the hospital, and it was touch-and-go for eight days. Then it got worse. They said she wouldn't make it. My husband, Don, said we had to let her go; but, because of losing my first child when I asked God to have His way, I was afraid to have that conversation again with Him. My husband said to me, "Do you trust God or not?" I didn't want God to take my baby away again! "Do you trust God or not?" Yes! I did trust God. We asked God to have His way, and within two days, Gail came home healthy.

I had terrible varicose veins in my legs; the pain would put me down. One time, we went to a church meeting and the preacher called me up for healing. When I went back to my seat, the pain was gone, and I knew God had healed me. At least I thought He did—until the next day! My legs were very swollen, and I was having more pain than I ever had before. The question came to me, "Do you believe you are healed and do you trust God?" The answer was yes, and I was immediately well!

About this time, we were a happy family of seven, plus two more kids (nephews) that we took in. My husband was a deacon in the church, and I was the church treasurer and Sunday school teacher. We also took care of the church and the church grounds. At that time, because I used my arms so much, painting fences and milking cows and things like that, my arms would fall asleep at night and keep me awake in pain. I got pretty rundown. The doctor said I should either take sleeping pills or a shot of whiskey at night. I didn't want to take the pills, so I took the whiskey.

Pretty soon, I was taking my shot of whiskey every two hours throughout the day, all day long, and whenever I thought I could get away with it. By now, it was vodka I was drinking because it had no smell, and I was drinking a bottle a day. Nobody knew. For some reason, I thought it was okay. I can't explain that, but I really thought it was okay. I guess that is called "justification." You know, "The doctor said…." Over a period of a few years, I became a "closet drinker." One day, as I was pouring myself a drink, it was the first and last time I actually heard God's audible voice. God said to me,

"Do you trust Me or not?" I said, "Yes, Lord, I do." He said, "If you pour the drink out and throw the bottle away, I'll help you and be with you. If you don't, you are on your own!" I threw it all away. I have never had a minute of wanting it or doing it again, not since that day. I did my part, and He did His!

My last child, Lori, was in high school when she had to have surgery. We were waiting in the hospital for the report, and the surgery was going to make it hard, if not impossible, for her to have children. My husband said to me as we were waiting, "We just have to trust God." About that time the doctor came out scratching his head, saying that he didn't know what happened, but that the tumor was gone; so they just sewed her back up!

A few years later, we were up in the mountains far from home and the phone rang. It was the hospital. They had called to tell us that Sandi, our fourth child, had been taken to Intensive Care, and it didn't look like she was going to make it. It was very serious. We couldn't get a flight out because of electrical storms and the wind, rain and lightning. The weather was shouting "No!" But, as usual, God had another plan. We went to a private airstrip to get a plane to go home, and the man who owned the airstrip said that we couldn't go up in that weather. He said it was too dangerous, and we couldn't do it. My husband, who had flown before, but didn't have his license, said, "Watch me!" He said, "The same God who made the storm can calm it and get us home safely." He was living the answer to the question, "Do you trust God or not?" Sandi was very sick and almost didn't make it through because of complications from her disease, but we made it back in time to rejoice over her triumph in Jesus.

> ***We have to trust God to know***
> ***that whatever comes our way, He will be with us and***
> ***give us strength to go through.***

Sometimes, it's just saying the name of Jesus when you're too sick to read or pray. Sometimes, it's crying your eyes out until you have no more tears. Sometimes, it's being still and knowing that God is

God. Sometimes it's just being quiet and feeling the sweet love of your friend, Jesus; knowing that you haven't done anything to deserve it, but it is still there, forever!

We have to trust God to know that whatever comes our way, He will be with us and give us strength to go through. He is in control. There's just no other way to live; I am proof of that! All those years ago, when the Salvation Army man prayed over me, I became a new creature. I didn't know it then, but I do know it now. I'm proud that He chose me to bring my family to Jesus.

The prayers of my brothers and sisters in Christ have always been there for me when I needed them. I know people have prayed for our family down through the years, and it has always mattered. The name of Jesus is all-powerful; He is closer than anyone or anything. All my children and their spouses are serving the Lord, along with all my grandchildren. This is a rare miracle when you consider where I came from! But then, that's just like the Lord, isn't it?

God's love is beyond our understanding. I just thank Him for it every day. I thank Him for being my friend and letting me be His friend. Praise You, my precious Jesus.

Yes, my mother, my friend, He walks with you, He talks with you and He tells you that you are His own.

My mother understands the power of friendship with the Lord. He is our purpose and our destination. There is no greater journey than to know Him. Moses is about to walk that out with a great price.

Moses has made a commitment that surpasses a fleeting conviction. I can picture his soul reaching upward as deep calls to deep to secure the friendship of the ages. As we commit to give our hopes and desires to the Lord, may we be found praying with Moses as he attempts to seal the heart of God upon his own.

Lord, I have discovered that, without trust, faith has no power. Teach me to walk in that trust no matter what the cost will be. Cause me to walk as a yielded vessel of forgiveness and honor. May my vision be clear and my heart pure as I go forward forsaking earthly purposes and mere flesh for Your presence. Amen.

PART THREE — THE FRIEND OF GOD

From the Exodus to the Exile

Learning to Learn

CHAPTER 18

Coming out to Become

As Israel is coming out of Egypt, I am reminded of a story that happened recently. While on a ministry tour, a friend was impressed with the snooze button on the hotel alarm clock. When I go to a hotel, I usually turn all the buttons off. But, for some reason, I didn't check this alarm clock to see if it had been set by the inmate who came before me. So, after a late night of ministry, the alarm went off at 5:30 a.m. I jumped out of bed and turned the alarm off, then I starting pacing the floor, praying. My friend, Kathleen, who was with me, began to shout with amazement, and I couldn't figure out what she was talking about.

She said, "That was the most fantastic display of 'get up and go' that I have ever seen!"

"What?" I replied, somewhat confused.

"I guess you don't understand," she said.

"Explain it to me," I said.

Kathleen proceeded to tell me that most everybody just hits the snooze button and lays there for a few more minutes, if not an entire hour.

"What?" I said again.

"Haven't you ever done that?" she asked.

"Why would I?" I said. "When the alarm goes off, you are supposed to get up!" Kathleen then told me that this is the state of Christianity; we all hit the "spiritual snooze button," and so we miss out on what the Lord is trying to tell us. She derived an entire teaching on spiritual complacency from this incident. Have you been hitting the "snooze button"?

The Israelites were. While Moses was being transformed from a mere man of Midian to a vessel whose identity was found in God alone, they were not hearing the sound of the alarm. Perhaps they thought just one more hour, just one more day, or just one more complaint of what will never be. They should have made their hearts ready, but they didn't. The time had now come, and they faced their destiny.

This man Moses was about ready for face-to-face fellowship with God. He was the one who, before too long, would be begging to see God's glory. He was the one who had evolved into a vessel that could trust. He was the vehicle that God would use to show people what obedience looked like. He is you and he is me; he is who the world is watching to see if they can trust God.

Although we are concentrating on Moses and his transformation from a man to a friend of God, it is hard to walk with him and not be amazed by some of the self-inflicted wounds of the Israelites. Their behavior on the road to the Red Sea is noteworthy, as they attempted to destroy Moses while he walked out his redemption from himself.

In chapter 13, God told them that He was taking them to the land that flowed with milk and honey. Not just the land of milk and honey, but the land that would be *flowing* with it! He proceeded to tell them that it was the land of the Canaanites, the Hittites, the Amorites, the Hivites and the Jebusites. They were barely out of Egypt, and God was reminding these people that this was the land that He promised to give to their fathers before them. He told them that they were going to talk about their journey someday, and when they did, this is what He wanted them to say: "This is the day that you came out of Egypt, out of the house of bondage; for by strength of hand the Lord brought you out from this place...." He told them to recite this to one another and to remind one another so they would never forget the great and mighty hand of the Lord. He told them to remind their children of how God redeemed them.

The Israelites were very aware of two things. First, that this was the promised land the Lord was taking them to. And second, that there would be giants in the land. The "ite" people who lived there were enemies of Israel, and many of them were giants. Many times, with great promises come great giants. Maybe the reason why Israel found contentment from time to time in Egypt was that they didn't want to fight the "ites." To walk in the promise, you have to fight the "ites." Often, there is no other way to do it. All through their story (much of which we will bypass), if they would have just remembered these two simple facts, things would have gone much better for them. But alas, they were a people who had created a destiny of delusion for themselves, and God knew it. As badly as God wanted to do it for them, He restrained Himself and gave them the opportunity to become what He was calling them to be—people of promise.

Faith and Trust
The people would go on a journey that would attempt to teach them trust. Moses was their example, and he was now walking straight; he was not crooked anymore! He was no longer deformed by the effects of rejection, but he would still need to perfect his trust as he obeyed God.

Moses learned that, no matter how bad it looked, no matter how many frogs were jumping around or how much hail was piling up on top of your head, when God makes a promise, He will perform it if you will show up to collect it!

As an example to the Israelites, Moses would have to be established as a man who obeyed his God in the face of situations that seemed out of control. Moses would be tempted to take matters into his own hands more than once. When he succumbed to the desire for control, he would fail; when he trusted God, he would succeed!

> *When he succumbed to the desire for control,*
> *he would fail; when he trusted God, he would succeed!*

The nation was watching this man, and it was making an attempt to walk in faith because of him. As we have seen, faith and trust are two different things. Trust is the element of maturity that is deposited into faith when you have something or someone you know you can count on. Trust has a confidence and a knowing to it. An unseen knowing is deposited into faith when you have trusted God for the outcome. Trust says, "It's about the journey, and I don't care where it takes me, I'm going with Jesus." The "man-made" kind of faith shouts to the outcome and dictates a result. Faith that doesn't have trust held within it cannot walk in fellowship. It will be so concerned about the end result that it will become proud and consumed with what it's trying to get. Life always puts regular faith to the test; it can't touch trust, for trust has been grounded in friendship, and its reward is great peace. That's the kind of faith that cannot be shaken! This is why, in scripture, peace is mentioned so often along with trust. When trust lies within your faith, there is no more struggle. Faith without trust is just an idea of the way you think it should be, but don't have the belief to truly hope for. "Thou wilt keep him in perfect peace, whose mind is stayed on thee: because he trusteth in thee" (Isaiah 26:3).

In order to be successful in the challenge that lay before them, the people would have to walk past faith and into a new thing: they would have to trust. Moses would attempt to walk a wide enough path for them to see how to get that done.

> And it came to pass, when Pharaoh had let the people go, that God led them not through the way of the land of the Philistines, although that was near; for God said, Lest peradventure the people repent when they see war, and they return to Egypt: But God led the people about, through the way of the wilderness of the Red sea: and the children of Israel went up harnessed out of the land of Egypt (Exodus 13:17–18).

This was the Israelites' opportunity to be trained to trust, and God would make every moment count. He would protect them from themselves by taking them the "long way around" to the promise. God was hovering, Moses was walking, but would the people move? The foundation of their failures was that they were cowards who craved comfort.

God knew their hearts were not prepared or sanctified unto Him and that they were not ready to pay the price to walk in total trust, but He kept hoping and giving them opportunity to turn from their choice of comfort and compromise. God never gives up on us.

God Designed the Battle

God knew there would be a battle; He designed it that way! Later in scripture, He talks about how He set them deliberately on that path so that Pharaoh would think he had them. Instead of responding to the Spirit, they reacted to the flesh, because they could not trust God. This was a maneuver that they would employ year after year.

God had made the announcement to them several times: "Watch what I can do, I am God! Check out how I am going to deliver you by My mighty power. Look at Moses, follow him as he teaches you to trust by his obedience." God was telling them to follow their leader as Moses followed God. He was saying to them, "I know you don't trust me because you don't really know me, I'm just somebody you've been complaining to for a very long time." When Paul said, "Follow me as I follow Christ," he was saying, "Look at me—I'm doing it, and so can you!" Paul didn't say to follow him, he said, "Follow God as you see me follow God." He was giving a living example of grace.

God purposefully caused the Israelites to camp on the edge of the wilderness in a very precarious position. God wanted the Egyptians to follow them, and they just couldn't wrap their minds around that idea.

As a testimony of His loving-kindness and care for His people, God manifested Himself in a special way when they were barely out of Egypt:

> *And the Lord went before them by day in a pillar of a*
> *cloud, to lead them the way; and by night in a pillar of*
> *fire, to give them light; to go by day and night: He took not*

away the pillar of the cloud by day, nor the pillar of fire by night, from before the people (Exodus 13:21–22).

And still, the people would spend the rest of their days doubting, and their occupation of choice was to complain.

The Great Drama of Redemption

God continued to reveal His plan in Exodus 14:3–4:

For Pharaoh will say of the children of Israel, They are entangled in the land, the wilderness hath shut them in. And I will harden Pharaoh's heart, that he shall follow after them; and I will be honoured upon Pharaoh and upon all his host; that the Egyptians may know that I am the Lord. And they did so.

So, along came Pharaoh and 600 of his best chariots and warriors. You can almost hear the excitement of God as He orchestrated this great drama of redemption. That's how God is about our trouble and pain; He is very excited about planning our deliverance. His plans always get Him the most honor and us the most benefit, but we have to allow Him to be God in our trouble and pain!

Honor is important to God. He wants the whole world to know He is the Lord. The situations that surround us should declare that God is in control, no matter how loudly they shout that He is not. God is not bound to our circumstances, but rather is consumed by the outcome beyond those circumstances. He will use our circumstances in order to declare to everyone that He is the Lord and He is in control. But so often in the middle of our circumstances, we shout louder than God, and what we are shouting is not that He is Lord!

Moses came to a place where he went beyond conviction and agreed with God. He was committed, but that commitment had the right to be proven. To walk in true commitment, we have to be able to trust God, or we will never be able to watch the Red Sea form walls around us. A mere conviction will be moved by confusion when the risk of losing comfort appears.

The battle lines were drawn. Pharaoh was almost right on top of the Israelites, and they began to panic. The Bible says they were afraid and cried out to the Lord. They yelled at Moses and accused him of tricking them by bringing them out of Egypt to be buried in the wilderness.

Were the plagues a faded memory already? Had the people so quickly forgotten the rigors of their old lifestyle? Did they truly miss the mud, the bricks, the sweat and the tears? Wasn't it just the other day that these guys were spreading blood on their doorposts, while every family in Egypt cried in horror as God Himself passed by and brought the reward for rebellion? What about the darkness that could be felt throughout the land, except by them? Couldn't they remember how God protected them during that time? What about the fire and cloud that were sitting right next to them? Didn't they realize that Pharaoh would have to plow through that first to get to them?

Moses was humbled by the power and provision that surrounded him. But the Israelites seemed to be indignant about it. They seemed to say, "It's not enough—we want more. And furthermore, we want you to do all the work!" However, Moses was learning to trust God in all things. He was walking in communion, which is agreement. The people he was leading didn't actually want to be led—that was their underlying problem. They simply wanted their own way. *This generation would not be able to fully trust because they were continually questioning God.* And then they went a step too far, in my book.

> *Is not this the word that we did tell thee in Egypt, saying, Let us alone, that we may serve the Egyptians? For it had been better for us to serve the Egyptians, than that we should die in the wilderness* (Exodus 14:12).

I had wondered what the Israelites were doing while Moses and Aaron were taking the heat over at the palace and the people were still in Egypt. While Moses was tearing up his flesh, learning how to be a vessel of God, these guys were complaining and telling him to leave them alone.

The Israelites were just told, in chapter 13, that God was taking them to the land that was flowing with milk and honey. God had just finished dealing with the Egyptians in a mighty way. Suddenly the Israelites were shouting at Moses, "We want to be Egyptian slaves!" This all happened because they were afraid, afraid of death. This fear of the unknown and fear of losing came from their inability to trust. Moses was trusting God, and he was their example, but they weren't paying attention. They were supposed to be the army of God. That is how God referred to them as they left Egypt. He said that they left in their "armies." What a horrible disappointment it must have been when they caved in so soon and began to behave as mice among men, instead of children of the Lion of Judah.

Couldn't they still see the bloody river and smell the dead frogs? Was the demonstration of who God was as fire and hail mixed with thunder, lightning and destructive rain that distant of a memory? Couldn't they still see the picture of the flies swarming and the locusts destroying everything in sight? Didn't they remember the screams of the Egyptians as their cattle died, their bodies were covered with boils and their firstborn children died? All of those things not only came from this God who was present in the pillar of fire in their camp, but it was the same God who brought deliverance from those plagues to all who called upon Him. Why couldn't they remember any of that? Because their fear was greater than their faith, and they were not willing to change that. By now, if they didn't believe God was who He said He was, they never would.

The statements that the Israelites made at this point, they would continue to make for the next 40 years. They were unhappy about leaving Egypt and they wanted to die. Bake it, fry it, broil it, barbeque it, saute it, burn it or serve it raw, but it is the same food—the food of apathy and compromise. It is the food that says, "Don't trust God," as you swallow it. It is who Moses was when he was a "bloody man" in Midian, trying to find a way around God. But he was no longer that man, for he had paid the price to become a vessel. He was willing to keep paying and learning in order to become a vessel of honor, forsaking the temptation to just be any old vessel.

Moses would bear with them until the end and even share their fate, for God had won his heart.

When we come "out of the world and into Christ," it's important to not just know what we came "out of," but to recognize what we are "going into." The Word says that we are "more than conquerors in Him" and that we are "overcomers in Him," which tells me that to do those things, we have to be "in Him." A redeemed man of God recently said, "I'm an alcoholic." No, he is not; he is redeemed! God saved and delivered him—that is now his new identity. Gaining identity from past sins or wounds is a perfect way to stay there. People who move on are willing to acknowledge that they are a "new creation in Christ Jesus," for all things have "become new!" Egypt represented the world, and if Israel was to ever fully trust God and walk in friendship with Him, they would have to stop declaring Egypt over themselves.

A Story of Deliverance

Years ago, when I was a child, there was a woman who came to the little church I attended in Vallejo, California. I remember her clearly, although I cannot remember her name. She told a story of passion and deliverance as if it had occurred yesterday. And I was shocked to learn that this incident had happened to her 12 years earlier.

She said that she had been a hopeless drug addict but was now a missionary. She had gone through every drug rehab program in the state of New York and had begun working on the rehab programs in Massachusetts when it happened. She was in jail on drug-related charges, and somebody came to see her. For years and years, while she had spent time in jail and detox, people always came to see her to try to "fix" her. She was the token "hopeless case." Many of these people had God and had a story similar to hers. Others didn't have God, but they had a program. Either way, every one of them could relate to her; but it meant nothing to her because they all seemed to find their identity in what they had done, rather than in who they had become.

Then it happened. She said a woman came to her cell holding a Bible, and this is the speech that the woman gave to her, the speech that changed her life:

I have never taken drugs before, and I don't know what that would be like. I can only imagine your pain and trials; clearly I have not had them. I have never been to jail, and I don't know anybody who has had your trouble. I have a nice little house and a nice little family, and we are very square. We go to church every Sunday, and my kids would never think of running away from home as early as you did! But this I know: the same Jesus who has kept me out of trouble all these years is the same Jesus who can bring you out and keep you out!

As this woman told her story in my church, her face lit up and her soul was visibly moved. She said that when the little, square church lady came to her cell 12 years ago, she knew God was big enough for her. If He could keep somebody from ever tasting of the world, then she knew there was hope for her. She needed a God that big. She said she was sick of people "relating" to her. She was saved and delivered that day. When she went to court, her demeanor had so dramatically changed that the judge removed all the charges against her. Then he told her to leave the state and go do what she said she was going to do for God and for others. She saw the mercy of God that day in the form of a miracle! We don't have to relate to people's sin; we just have to relate to God, the One who keeps us!

Moses was able to walk past Egypt, in all its splendor and horror, because he was willing to live as a new man. Egypt held many things for Moses—good memories and bad. But he was no longer getting his identity from his state as a prince or a pauper in Egypt—he was God's. His wound and pain would no longer be his identity. This was not about possessing the future or the land; it was about possessing the promise, the promise of friendship with God.

Moses came out of Egypt to become the friend of God. It wasn't easy, and I don't believe it was supposed to be easy. The road to Canaan had a high cost. For Moses, it wasn't about "coming out;" he was perfectly content in Midian. For Moses, it was not about what the trade-off was; he was not trading Midian for Canaan. Canaan was the promise for the people, not Moses. And the people would do what they wanted with that promise. But Moses had something far deeper and richer on his mind: fellowship with a Friend. When we leave our Egypt, we need to have already made the decision that the trade is worth it. We trade who we are for who Christ is by learning to lean on Him.

Perhaps you can't get past who you were yesterday because it's all you know. Maybe it's a safe and secure place because it's home to you. But God has called you to this new place: the place of abundance in Him. You are not the same person you were when you started the journey of this book. You have changed, and so has your emotional address.

CHAPTER 19

The Visible Vessel

And the Lord said unto Moses, Wherefore criest thou unto me? Speak unto the children of Israel, that they go forward.... (Exodus 14:15)

God reminded Moses that he was a vessel, not a mere man who could be manipulated by the cries and accusations of people. God was telling him, "You know what I'm doing; they don't, but you do!" God was telling Moses to rise up and behave like a "vessel of honor." He said, "Don't go back and be the man you were in Egypt or Midian." God was saying, "Don't respond to them—respond to Me!" Who we respond to is an indicator of who we are friends with. Oh, the horror of forgetting what God is doing!

Next, God reminded Moses that He was going to force the Egyptians to chase the Israelites so that He could get honor from Pharaoh, his men, his chariots, and even his horses. God was going to finish Pharaoh off with style!

It's God's declaration of parenthood over us. No matter what we are going through, God will always assume the position of protector over His children.

And the angel of God, which went before the camp of Israel, removed and went behind them; and the pillar of the cloud went from before their face, and stood behind them:

And it came between the camp of the Egyptians and the camp of Israel; and it was a cloud and darkness to them, but it gave light by night to these: so that the one came not near the other all the night (Exodus 14:19–20).

God is always in the middle of defending you, even when it looks like He has forgotten you. God is standing in the middle of the war even before it starts. He has drawn the battle lines Himself; nothing is an accident concerning you. He is in between His children and their enemy. The same presence that brought darkness to the enemy brought light for the Israelites. Even though they didn't get it, even though they didn't deserve it, God was still busy being God and taking care of them.

When we are going through our grief and trouble, we can't always see the pillar of fire between us and the enemy. That's when the "knowing" comes in handy. What did God say? Remember that and hold on to it; believe it, and all will be well with our souls. The Israelites often made an occupation out of getting confused on this issue. Perhaps "one came not near the other all the night" because the Israelites were attempting to go back, just as the Egyptians were attempting to go forward! The Lord was busy protecting them even from themselves. Oh, how they longed to go back to Egypt where the "livin' was easy!" But then, that wasn't really the truth, was it? Their current state of fear and mistrust had suddenly convinced them that slavery was free and painless. There was an open revolt in the land, and the Lord went to great measures to show them they could trust Him, but would they?

They soon forgot His works; they waited not for His counsel: But lusted exceedingly in the wilderness, and tempted God in the desert (Psalm 106:13–14).

When we can't see the other side of the Red Sea, sometimes the shouting we do is not about victory, but about fear! Believing before our victory comes is a lifestyle of trust. Shouting victory on this side of the Red Sea is something that a friend would do. Shouting victory on this side of the Red Sea is something that can only be done by someone whose spiritual eyes are opened. Shouting victory on this side of the Red Sea can only be done when we trust and don't have to see it to believe it. The Israelites' eyes were small because their mouths were too big! Moses, on the other hand, was daring to believe. He was daring to travel from God's hand to His face. Moses, in just a moment, was going to make a leap of faith that would forever change his identity. He would obey because he could trust. Open our eyes, Lord, that we may know Your redemption when the earth around us is shaking.

In 2 Kings, Elisha deals with spiritual blindness in power and confidence.

> *And when the servant of the man of God was risen early, and gone forth, behold, an host compassed the city both with horses and chariots. And his servant said unto him, Alas, my master! how shall we do? And he answered, Fear not: for they that be with us are more than they that be with them. And Elisha prayed, and said, Lord, I pray thee, open his eyes, that he may see. And the Lord opened the eyes of the young man; and he saw: and, behold, the mountain was full of horses and chariots of fire round about Elisha. And when they came down to him, Elisha prayed unto the Lord, and said, Smite this people, I pray thee, with blindness. And he smote them with blindness according to the word of Elisha (2 Kings 6:15–18).*

It was easy for Elisha to pray that prayer, because he had a knowing! A desire for the things of the Spirit will eventually give way to the knowing of the things of the Spirit. Elisha knew his God, so he knew what his God would do. He not only knew what his God was doing, but he wasn't afraid to participate in it. That's the stuff of friends, and that's the land where Moses was just about to secure an address.

Going Forward
Moses told the people to "go forward" as God had commanded him to do, and God sent clouds and fire to babysit them. Then in

175

the middle of the night, God asked Moses to do something that would take perseverance, fortitude and heart. It would change the way that everyone looked at God throughout history. A mere man could not have done it, but a vessel striving to become the friend of God would run to it. This time, Moses obeyed without questioning!

> *And Moses stretched out his hand over the sea; and the Lord caused the sea to go back by a strong east wind all that night, and made the sea dry land, and the waters were divided. And the children of Israel went into the midst of the sea upon the dry ground: and the waters were a wall unto them on their right hand, and on their left* (Exodus 14:21–22).

In the middle of a dark and windy night, this man would have to believe in order to receive. Trust would have to be lodged deep within his faith. Trust and faith, as we have seen, are different. I'm sure Moses knew God could part the Red Sea; but knowing He would do it when Moses obeyed, when Moses needed Him to, would take trust! While tornado-force winds swirled around Moses, he would have to stand against the odds and against a complaining people and an approaching enemy who was bringing an incoming battle. This was the same east wind that blew for a day and a night to bring in the locusts. The old familiar whistle in the air had returned. What will you believe and trust God for in the midst of that horrible, wonderful, frightening wind? We know He can part the Red Sea, but we often wonder, "Will He do it for me?"

To make matters worse, Moses didn't have to just stand; he had to stand with his arms stretched out over the sea all night long. The Lord Himself was holding the enemy off at the cloud of darkness while Moses acted out his heart for God in a rare display of obedience. Why did Moses have to stand all night long with his arms stretched out over a huge sea with a mighty wind pushing at his back? Because God gave him a promise, that's why! When God gives us a promise, a time will come when we must persevere in it until it is performed. When we allow the enemy to steal our promise because of our own unbelief or tired soul, when we walk with a lack of trust, we have allowed him to call God unfaithful. If you can't hold on for yourself or those around you, hold on for the honor of God!

God is right in the middle of our trouble, "making a way where there is no way."

God is right in the middle of our trouble, "making a way where there is no way." Life brings wind; God brings direction to that wind. Life brings rain; God brings purpose to that rain. Life brings fire; God brings redemption right in the middle of it. God comes with a mighty force to fulfill the promise He made to us. Sometimes, like it or not, that takes a powerful east wind to accomplish—even if we don't like the wind. The wind is inconvenient at times and unpredictable, but it is necessary, as God begins to present the perfection of the promise that we have been waiting for. The water is troubled before miracles emerge, the fire becomes its hottest just before the refining process is complete, and sometimes wind blows in the fiercest of gales when it's ready to drop the answer upon you.

Moses Had Changed
What of Moses and the long night? There he was, stretching his hands out all night long. How long did he stand there with nothing happening? When the wind came, how long did it blow before the water began to move? Did the people think God was sending more locusts upon them? When Moses first stood there, looking at the sea in the middle of the night, did he wonder if God would back him up or not? Did he wonder if he had really heard God, or would this be a replay of his earlier disappointment in Egypt? Or did he know, beyond a shadow of a doubt, that he was truly accepted and no longer rejected?

Only heaven holds the answers to many of these questions. But this I do know: the man standing with his hands stretched out across the Red Sea was a different man than the one who sat at the well in Midian and pondered his plight. Moses had only faint memories of who he was before, because now he was standing with the I AM, and all things had "become new." Here in this moment, he knew, without a doubt, that he had found the God he raced out of Egypt 40 years ago to find. In a few minutes, the dry ocean bed lying at his feet would forever remind him that he could trust God to bring abundance upon his obedience.

There is no record of Moses worrying about looking like an idiot if God didn't show up for him. He never flinched. If he asked any questions or had any concerns, they were the wanderings of everyman, of you and me. But in all that wondering (if he, in fact, wondered at all), he never disgraced his God as he stood before that huge mass of water, with the enemy closing in on him. He was apparently consumed by "going with God"! There is no record of Moses complaining that he was cold, tired, thirsty, hungry, old or scared. There is no record of Moses doing anything except obeying this God that he had become committed to. Abundance will always come from obedience. Remember, just because you are still waiting for God to accomplish what He said He would, it doesn't mean He's late; it only means that you are still waiting, and He's on the way!

> *And Moses stretched out his hand over the sea; and the Lord caused the sea to go back by a strong east wind all that night, and made the sea dry land, and the waters were divided. And the children of Israel went into the midst of the sea upon the dry ground: and the waters were a wall unto them on their right hand, and on their left* (Exodus 14:21–22).

Look what happened next. The sea not only went back, but it was divided, and the ground beneath the sea was dry. (When God does a thing, He really does a thing!) Imagine crossing the Red Sea with dust beneath your feet and dry sand about you, while walls of water are on either side of you. I wonder if the fish jumped from one wall to the other, flying over the heads of those who were making the crossing. I can only imagine the "show" that went on that night!

Walkway of Glory

This was a walkway of glory as far as the eye could see—it was holy ground! The Bible doesn't say what was keeping the walls of water upright. It doesn't say that the wind was still present. You get the idea that it had already left, because later in scripture, Moses is told to simply "stretch out (your) hand over the sea that the waters may return." The sheer, raw power of the God who created all things is leaning on the wall of water. What an experience that must have been!

The water dividing doesn't catch my attention nearly as much as the fact that the people walked across on dry ground. God had addressed every last detail; each care and concern had been researched. Every point of contention had been removed. Shadrach, Meshach and Abednego came out of the fire and didn't even smell of smoke. Jonah came out of the belly of the fish and was in one piece. Daniel went to the lions' den and seemingly had a "nap." Joseph was thrown in a pit and emerged as second-in-command over the whole of Egypt. Jesus suffered Calvary and rose up in victory. You may have gone through hell and back upon this earth, but look at you—you are still standing!

Reverend Joe Albright of www.dialhope.org tells the following story about the interaction between Charlton Heston and Cecil B. DeMille regarding the chariot race in the film of Ben Hur:

> When they began working on the movie *Ben Hur*, DeMille talked to Charlton Heston, the star of the movie, about the chariot race scene. He decided that rather than using a stunt double, Heston should actually learn to drive the chariot himself. Heston agreed to take chariot-driving lessons to make the movie as authentic as possible.
>
> This was no small feat! Learning to drive a chariot pulled by four powerful horses, was an enormous challenge. After extensive work and days of practice, Heston returned to the movie set and reported to DeMille. He said, "I think I can drive the chariot all right, Cecil, but I'm not at all sure I can actually win the race."

With a slight smile on his face, DeMille said, "Heston, you just stay in the race, and I'll make sure you win."

And that's how it is with God, the great Director of life: If we just show up, there is no telling what He will do!

People are desperate for hope. They will go just about anywhere and do anything to get it. Just as Moses had to simply keep "showing up" and "stay in the race," so to speak, we, too, have to keep pursuing the Lord in the middle of times that are so hard that we would rather give up. Those are the times when our "vesselhood" is under scrutiny. Those are the times when the world is judging us and hoping, at the same time, that what we have is actually real and big enough to weather a storm. Believe it or not, they are rooting for us, because they would love a dose of something that works. The world is watching you. So make sure they get a godly show, because they may never turn your channel on again!

CHAPTER 20

God Will Be Glorified

And the Egyptians pursued, and went in after them to the midst of the sea, even all Pharaoh's horses, his chariots, and his horsemen. And it came to pass, that in the morning watch the Lord looked unto the host of the Egyptians through the pillar of fire and of the cloud, and troubled the host of the Egyptians (Exodus 14:23–24).

Right when you think you can't take anymore, here come the Egyptians! When you think it's time to get delivered, it seems like God thinks it's time to dig in! The Egyptians had chariots. Surely they were gaining quickly on the Israelites. But as I sit and think about this scene, I wonder why 600 chariots and horsemen would be a threat to millions of people who were aided by a God not afraid to throw plagues out at people and deliver those whom He loved by a mighty hand filled with miracles? I believe it's because they did not truly know or trust God. They merely knew of Him and watched Him do what He did, but never really understood why He did any of it. They could not grasp that He was delivering them, not because of who they were, but because of who He is. The lack of that knowledge would cost them Canaan as time would go by.

The Egyptians followed the Israelites into the "midst of the sea." They were playing for keeps. They would chase the Israelites until they could see the whites of their eyes. And, at first, the water didn't move. The wall fashioned by God seemed to be protecting the enemy too. That's how it appears sometimes. But God says, "Don't get upset when it looks like evil is prospering and prevailing...the day will come, trust Me!" Jeremiah 29:11 is timeless: "For I know the thoughts that I think toward you, saith the Lord, thoughts of peace, and not of evil, to give you an expected end."

What on earth would provoke the Egyptians to waltz down Aquarium Avenue anyway? Hadn't they seen the plagues, didn't the firstborn in each of their homes die? Couldn't they still feel that creepy, cold darkness enveloping them? They forgot who they were coming up against. They underestimated the power of God responding to His love for His people. They thought they were chasing mere people, but they weren't; they were chasing the people of God. Hatred and anger will provoke you to do the stupidest things!

And God Moved

The Lord waited for just the right moment before He moved away from the wall of water. Pharaoh didn't just go in after the Israelites, he went in after them with all he had, and God was waiting for him there.

And then God looked at the Egyptians. And all it took was one look! This is the God who was defending His people. There He was, in all His splendor, looking at their enemy right through the pillar of fire and smoke that had been surrounding them all this time. It's not enough that the water had divided and the ocean had been turned into vertical walls on either side of them. Forget about the fact that they walked across on dry ground. Here we have the face of God looking at their enemy through this gigantic skyscraper of fire with one thing on His mind: to trouble their enemy! And trouble them He did.

It was early in the morning, and the Almighty had made a plan for the day: to trouble the Egyptians. I'd like to know exactly what the word "trouble" means. *Strong's Exhaustive Concordance* defines "trouble" (*hamam*, #H2000) like this: "To put in commotion... disturb...break...crush, destroy." The *New American Standard*

Exhaustive Concordance says it means "to make a noise, move noisily, confuse, discomfit."

This was a rattling, shaking, horrifying episode. Every type of disturbance that God could drum up, He was going to use. He was the God of thunder and lighting, fire and hail. He was the God who commanded the wind and created lice from dust and blood from thin air. He could, most clearly, do anything He wanted in order to fulfill His own definition of "troubled."

The Egyptians would have a single moment of clarity in which they would realize that no one can get between God and His children and win. Let us venture forward and really see what "troubled" looks like to God, as He paints a picture for us through the pillar of fire:

> *And [He] took off their chariot wheels, that they drave them heavily: so that the Egyptians said, Let us flee from the face of Israel; for the Lord fighteth for them against the Egyptians. And the Lord said unto Moses, Stretch out thine hand over the sea, that the waters may come again upon the Egyptians, upon their chariots, and upon their horsemen. And Moses stretched forth his hand over the sea, and the sea returned to his strength when the morning appeared; and the Egyptians fled against it; and the Lord overthrew the Egyptians in the midst of the sea. And the waters returned, and covered the chariots, and the horsemen, and all the host of Pharaoh that came into the sea after them; there remained not so much as one of them* (Exodus 14:25–28).

And Moses Moved with God

Notice the monument to human change that has taken place: Moses is silent. He is the servant who became a son, the son who would become the friend. Just as trust is mature faith, a friend is a mature vessel. These elements of spiritual evolution are seen in our everyday lives: a child is born and learns to obey, grows and learns to serve, becomes an adult and learns to walk in responsibility of who he/she has become. To become a friend of God is not about Canaan; it's about the promise of Canaan. It's not about what we get, but about who we become. It's not about how disappointed we are with God or our situation; it's about the level of intimacy we are willing to walk in with Him. It's about trusting Jesus, no matter how many times the well runs dry or the meat is all gone!

Because of the great turmoil and trial that surrounded the Israelites, God was able to bring great triumph. Moses wasn't watching anymore; he was participating! He was not standing against God anymore; he was moving with Him!

The Lord took the wheels off their chariots, and the Egyptians began to give God what He was after—honor! They shouted as they drove their chariots into the hard ground, "Let us flee from the face of Israel; for the Lord fights for them against the Egyptians." Their moment of clarity had now come and gone. The noise of God taking the wheels off their chariots and the rumble of the water as it descended upon them were the last things they heard before chaos and destruction came upon them.

Moses and the Israelites had crossed the Red Sea. They were standing on the shore, and God instructed Moses just like He did before; but this time it was in the wee hours of the morning. "Stretch your hand out over the sea," is what Moses was told to do. When Moses obeyed, the waters came upon the Egyptians, upon their chariots, and upon their horsemen. A mighty tumult of God's ocean descended upon the entire army as it chased the Israelites into their freedom. Not one of them remained. Now, that is complete and total deliverance!

Then "the sea returned to his strength when the morning appeared; and the Egyptians fled against it; and the Lord overthrew the Egyptians in the midst of the sea."

What was Moses doing throughout this scene? Again, he was waiting in obedience for the answer to come. Just imagine standing there with a multitude of God's people behind you. They aren't just any people; they are the people who just told you off. They are the people who are fearful and insecure and lazy. These people are the worst part of who you used to be. If there was any doubt in Moses, it better be gone now. To operate as one who is carrying the will of God around on his sleeve, there is no room for extra baggage. This is his defining moment. Will he falter; will he flee? Will he argue or complain? He is surrounded by people who, at any given moment, would. But will he? Who has he become? Is he a man or a vessel? Will he ever walk close enough to this God to be different from all other men, or is "normal" going to be okay? Will he ever forsake himself long enough to touch the face of God? And if he does, will arrogance overcome him?

Once we have overcome, if we have rejection in our soul, arrogance can rise up to protect and defend that rejection. It will puff you up so you don't have to feel your rejection, and a false sense of security will rest upon you. This is why it was so critical for Moses to deal with his rejection issues, along with the fear and insecurity that they produced, before he faced the Red Sea as a vessel of God. As a man, his arms would have been tired and his heart heavy, but as a vessel of God, he would be consumed with only one thought in the middle of his obedience: "I trust my God!"

The people he was traveling with could not shout "Glory!" on that side of the Red Sea, but perhaps, after God proved Himself yet one more time, they would be able to shout it on this side. Moses raised his hand as the Egyptians approached. The water was still not moving, and the Egyptians were just about to the shore. Moses had no time to wonder if he had heard God now, and there was no desire to argue with Him. As a vessel of God, you will be able to look at impending doom and forsake its foreboding thoughts of destruction.

The people he was leading cried and screamed in dismay, no doubt, for they were not a people of belief but a people of mere purpose. *Sometimes, purpose can fight belief. It can become a cheap substitute, if we are not careful.* They were God's people, and that was their purpose—to be God's people. But, to do that well, they had to go beyond purpose and walk into belief that lent itself to faith. That can only happen if you are willing to trust the One who has called you to the purpose that lies in front of you.

Moses kept his hand stretched out until the dawn broke. We don't know how long this was, but this we do know: Moses did not fail.

He had been qualified to become a friend of God because he was willing to believe the faithfulness of God to the point of his own destruction, and that's friendship. It is the "no matter what" kind of faith, the kind that increases with every tragedy and trial. It is the kind of faith that gets excited with each and every move of the enemy toward it. This faith makes us sure of one thing: God will get honor from the trial. When you carry that kind of faith, you don't care about your own deliverance anymore, you only care about His honor and glory being given and known. When you carry that kind of faith, you will trust your Friend for anything and gladly walk with Him through fire. And even water!

Midian seems like it was so long ago! It is hard to imagine that Moses ever wore the royal apparel of Egypt, doesn't it? It would appear today that the insecurities of a man standing before Pharaoh's court never even happened. When God says He's going to do something, He will do it, even if He has to get past palaces and sheep and people who forget their destiny!

Moses succeeded in his quest for perfect obedience, and the people were brought to silence as a mighty torrent of water reclaimed the ocean floor. No tsunami, no earthquake, no rain or hail, just a mighty God moving through fire, water and clouds to honor and defend His friend, Moses. There would be no trouble from the Red Sea that day upon the children that Moses told to be still. God was in complete control.

> *Thus the Lord saved Israel that day out of the hand of the Egyptians; and Israel saw the Egyptians dead upon the sea shore. And Israel saw that great work which the Lord did upon the Egyptians: and the people feared the Lord, and believed the Lord, and his servant Moses* (Exodus 14:30–31).

It had been quite a year for Moses. He had been dwelling in Midian, minding his own business, when the burning bush changed his life. He had wandered from there over to Egypt and got out of his "comfort zone." He ducked plagues and held onto promises and finally stood on the shore of an ocean that redesigned itself at his command. Yes, it was quite a year for Moses, and God was proud of him. He had walked over the top of the dead bodies and kept going forward.

> *He was willing to believe the faithfulness of God*
> *to the point of his own destruction.*

Exodus chapter 15 is the song the people sang with Moses as a triumphant shout unto the Lord after they safely crossed the Red Sea. As they rejoiced in God's great victory, they sang:

The Song of Moses

> *[The Lord] hath triumphed gloriously: the horse and his rider hath He thrown into the sea. The Lord is my strength and song, and He has become my salvation: he is my God, and I will prepare Him an habitation; my father's God, and I will exalt Him. The Lord is a man of war: the Lord is his name.*
>
> *Pharaoh's chariots and his host hath He cast into the sea: his chosen captains also are drowned in the Red Sea. The depths have covered them: they sank into the bottom as a stone. Thy right hand, O Lord, is become glorious in power: thy right hand, O Lord, hath dashed in pieces the enemy. And in the greatness of thine excellency thou hast overthrown them that rose up against thee: thou sentest forth thy wrath, which consumed them as stubble. And with the blast of thy nostrils the waters were gathered together, the floods stood upright as an heap, and the depths were congealed in the heart of the sea. The enemy said, I will pursue, I will over-take, I will divide the spoil; my lust shall be satisfied upon them; I will draw my sword, my hand shall destroy them. Thou didst blow with thy wind, the sea covered them: they sank as lead in the mighty waters.*

Who is like unto thee, O Lord, among the gods? Who is like thee, glorious in holiness, fearful in praises, doing wonders? Thou stretchedst out thy right hand, the earth swallowed them. Thou in thy mercy hast led forth the people which thou hast redeemed: thou hast guided them in thy strength unto thy holy habitation. The people shall hear, and be afraid: sorrow shall take hold on the inhabitants of Palestina. Then the dukes of Edom shall be amazed; the mighty men of Moab, trembling shall take hold upon them; all the inhabitants of Canaan shall melt away. Fear and dread shall fall upon them; by the greatness of thine arm they shall be as still as a stone; till thy people pass over, O Lord, till the people pass over, which thou hast purchased.

Thou shalt bring them in, and plant them in the mountain of thine inheritance, in the place, O Lord, which thou hast made for thee to dwell in, in the Sanctuary, O Lord, which thy hands have established. The Lord shall reign for ever and ever. For the horse of Pharaoh went in with his chariots and with his horsemen into the sea, and the Lord brought again the waters of the sea upon them; but the children of Israel went on dry land in the midst of the sea.... Sing ye to the Lord, for He hath triumphed gloriously; the horse and his rider hath He thrown into the sea. (Exodus 15:1-21)

The "Song of Moses" is a beautiful declaration of who God became to Moses. It is a sonnet to his maker and keeper, a poem that exclaims not only who God is, but who Moses had become. This is a vessel who was being rewarded with friendship because he was able to trust God. When God has a habitation in our hearts, we can trust Him. Friendship emerges from that habitation.

Have you noticed what Moses did? He made a declaration to God that would forever change him. Moses made a choice, and the choice mattered. This was the beginning of his decision to walk in trust and not hide behind excuses. An excuse will say, "There is a rational cause that I am this way. I am a product of the past and I have to behave this way. Because of who I was, I cannot change. I am this way because of my past, and it's okay!" But a reason will say, "This is why I have behaved this way and I recognize it, despise it and shall fix it. Regardless of my past, I will not dishonor God or my future." Reasons will find a way to be recognized and reconciled because they are resting upon a person who wants to go forward in God and hasn't been able to help himself before. Excuses rest upon a person who is validated by his wounds and gladly victimized over and over again to maintain his excuse for not changing and not going forward in God. Moses walked past excuses, reconciled reasons, and made a powerful declaration of God in himself. Moses became qualified that day.

Moses declared in this song that he would prepare God a new habitation, even a sanctuary. He was declaring that he was done with who he was and that he would willingly, knowingly not only embrace God, but forsake his old ways and who he used to be. Often we embrace who God is, but forget to let go of who we once were.

This song follows the progress of the life of Moses. You give God a "habitation" in your heart when you are walking in obedience. You give Him a "holy habitation" when you are walking as a vessel of God. But when you make a "sanctuary" in your heart for Him, you are walking in friendship with Him.

So, I guess the question is, "Does God have a one-room apartment in our hearts or does He have a mansion there?" The Bible tells us that we are "the temple of the Holy Ghost," the "people of God's habitation," a "strong habitation" for the Lord. In the song in Exodus 15, we are told to prepare a habitation for the Lord in our hearts. First Kings 8 talks about "a settled and sacred place for God to dwell in forever." That shouts at us across the ages and says, "That's you!" Galatians 5 asks the question, "How important is a spirit-led life to us?" Further, we are told in Isaiah 54 to "enlarge our tents and stretch the curtains of our habitation." Our heart belongs to us, it is ours; but will we make room for God there and then give it to Him, so He can create a sanctuary out of it?

Stretching and remodeling is messy at times, and it hurts. It's not about if you succeed or fail; it's about if you are willing to let God have enough control to make you holy, enough control to separate you from the world and enough control to be your Friend. Clearly, it's not about succeeding or failing, it's about gaining Christ.

God went to great lengths to gain glory. He said over and over again that He would receive glory and honor from the situation. He is a big God, and so He enjoys presenting big solutions to those who have big trust factors. Gideon's army had to be reduced to a small band a fraction of the size of the enemy, or the glory would have been too small to appeal to God. Daniel was always pushing the odds because he knew that God was bigger than he was. David was always biting off more than he could chew in battle because he knew that God called him to the war and hand-selected those battles for His own glory. Without a trial, there would never be a triumph; so we should get excited when trials come, knowing what they produce!

When you are walking with your Friend or waiting upon Him, it is never about the destination, but always about the journey. How good it is to wait upon the Lord, finding new ways to prepare yourself for Him, so that His arriving will be that much sweeter. How good it is to walk with the Lord, finding new ways to enjoy the journey that He has especially selected just for you. And if it hasn't been good for you, then find out why, because your walk with Christ is not supposed to be torturous. It is supposed to be amazing and triumphant!

CHAPTER 21

Take Me
to the Mountain

*So Moses brought Israel from the Red Sea, and they went
out into the wilderness of Shur; and they went three days
in the wilderness, and found no water. And when they
came to Marah, they could not drink of the waters of Marah, for they were bitter: therefore the name of it was called
Marah. And the people murmured against Moses, saying,
What shall we drink?* (Exodus 15:22–24)

People, people, people…please! Get to the back of the train and
be quiet! They should have secured a copyright on that song
they were just singing in the last chapter and played it a little
longer and a little louder so that they could actually believe what they
were singing! It seems that they had been so wrapped up in the beat,
they never heard the words. It was the song of Moses, and they hadn't
made it their own. They didn't "pay" for it, they simply wanted to sing
it. Evidently, the words were still meaningless to them. Matthew 15:8
says, "This people draweth nigh unto me with their mouth, and me
with their lips; but their heart is far from me."

Three short days after the parting of the waters, and they had already forgotten why the ocean mist had been upon their faces back

there. By now, you'd think that the people would be excited about tragedy. They had gone through the school of "tragedy training," and knew what tragedy could do—bring triumph and victory. But they were continually refusing to walk that out. Before its time, Romans 8:28 was being worked out in the life of Moses. "All things work together for good to them that love God, to them who are the called according to his purpose." If you study it out, the literal meaning for "good" here goes like this: to make you worthy and valuable for the work and to be honorable in it for the Lord. Moses has evolved from being a goodly child to a goodly man in the widest sense of the word.

We would do well to practice the Exodus 15 song on the other side of the Red Sea before the water moves. Perhaps then, we'd believe it. It doesn't really count when you can only sing it after the deliverance comes. That's relief, not belief! When we can only sing it on this side of the Red Sea, it's not part of us—it's just a happy song; it's upon the skin around our bones, but not in our bones because it doesn't go that deep. "Faith is the substance of things hoped for and the evidence of things not seen." Oh, to have the faith of a friend, the faith that Moses had developed. The Israelites never took the time to develop true faith, so they didn't have any. They never took the time to learn how to get past themselves and walk with God, so they were always limping and struggling. We are made to resemble and reflect God, not mankind. Let that be our identity forever. We were not made to walk in the afflictions of man but in the aspirations of God. We have already overcome the battle in Him. Now, we need to walk like it.

The people had sung of the greatness of God and they had even sung about how the Canaanites would "melt away." But this was information that they couldn't seem to hold onto. Every few days, they would forget about it. They even forgot about it when they were standing on the Canaan county line. Like I said before, they were continually forgetting who they were and what they were called to do. They were in the spiritual spin cycle: Sin, Sorry, Salvation. Sin, Sorry, Salvation. It never seemed to end. It would go on for years.

First, they were mad at Moses because there was only bitter water to drink. So God supernaturally made the water sweet.

Then, they walked a little further and the whole congregation murmured against Moses and said that they wished that God had just killed them when they were back in Egypt, because at least there, they had decent food to eat. The people refused to allow their flesh to suffer for even a moment. Their lack of discipline allowed a hungry compromise into their lives. All this complaining, and they had barely started on their journey. This went on for what seems like ages. There was never a miracle that was big enough for them.

Their song definitely ended quickly, the romance was over, and the honeymoon came to a screeching halt. Thirsty, hungry, unsure in frustrating, perilous times—all perfectly ordained by God to do one thing: teach them to trust! They had to believe God for their protection, their provision and their purpose; but they could not trust Him. Each day they had to inquire of God to survive. He planned it that way, for this was the school of Life in the Spirit for Israel. God was busy taking time to teach the people how to trust. He instructed them with vivid life applications in an effort to compel them to know that He was trustworthy. But they were afflicted with their own desires and abilities, so they wouldn't listen, and they refused to learn. At the end of the day, we will only do what we want to do, no matter how great the lesson or the teacher. The people refused to alter their "wanting," so they always came up lacking.

At Mount Sinai

Let's fly by the spin cycle that Israel seemed to be stuck in and move forward to get a look at the people with Moses at the base of Mount Sinai. For Moses, there was a sweet song being played. It was a song that he sang to himself about the faithfulness of his Friend—a song without words. The struggles of the infancy of faith no longer existed. He walked right over to the mountain without a shake or a quake in his soul.

> *And the Lord said unto Moses, Go unto the people, and sanctify them to day and to morrow, and let them wash their clothes, And be ready against the third day: for the*

*third day the Lord will come down in the sight of all the
people upon mount Sinai (Exodus 19:10–11).*

The people were told to prepare for the day. On the third day, what
a beautiful sound they were permitted to hear! Moses was told to
sanctify the people before God. This is the same sanctification that
Moses had undergone, and "to sanctify" (*qadash*, #H6942) means
to "consecrate, dedicate...holy." God was saying that the people
needed to prepare to show themselves dedicated and holy before
Him so that they would be qualified to see His glory. Unfortunately,
they weren't interested in seeing anything but their own pleasures
and comfort come to pass.

The story continues with Moses attempting to sanctify the people
and wash their clothes. But God knew that their hearts had fences
around them. Those fences would soon build a fence between them
and the glory of God. They were satisfied at the base of the mountain and had no desire to see the glory of God, let alone touch it. A
lack of radical obedience will do that to you—it will cause a satisfaction to come upon you that you have no business experiencing.
That satisfaction will cause you to be unwilling to prepare yourself
for greatness, and eventually it will rob you of God's glory, and His
favor will elude you.

To touch the glory of God with an unprepared heart spells
our spiritual death. It can come in many forms. It can come as
a lack of respect for holy things, a disregard for repentance, or
a disconnection from the Lord's abiding presence that provokes
us toward Him.

To Israel, this death would be literal if they violated God's command on the third day. They still had too much of Egypt in them,
and God could smell it. They were looking toward God but were
ready to turn and run at any given moment, and God knew it. They
had "washed" but not "sanctified," and it showed!

**The people needed to show themselves
dedicated and holy before Him
so that they would be qualified to see His glory.**

Moses Was Qualified

As for Moses, he stood firm as a man consumed with something bigger than himself. He had been qualified because he was willing to trust God. A mere man would run, not knowing what would happen to him at the base of a smoking, thundering mountain. A simple vessel would have become confused; but this man, this vessel of honor who had a Friend, would stand and see the redemption of his God.

> *And it came to pass on the third day in the morning, that there were thunders and lightnings, and a thick cloud upon the mount, and the voice of the trumpet exceeding loud; so that all the people that was in the camp trembled. And Moses brought forth the people out of the camp to meet with God; and they stood at the nether part of the mount. And mount Sinai was altogether on a smoke, because the Lord descended upon it in fire: and the smoke thereof ascended as the smoke of a furnace, and the whole mount quaked greatly. And when the voice of the trumpet sounded long, and waxed louder and louder, Moses spake, and God answered him by a voice. And the Lord came down upon mount Sinai, on the top of the mount: and the Lord called Moses up to the top of the mount; and Moses went up* (Exodus 19:16–20).

What a sight, what a sound, what a moment that must have been! The people were trembling, but not Moses. He was ready to climb the mountain.

When the Lord comes down, He always calls you up. If you don't know He came down, you won't be able to hear Him call you up. Mary of Bethany had that figured out. In Luke 10, Martha and Mary were working in the house. When Jesus entered the room, Mary set everything else aside. She was done doing dishes! Martha complained, and Jesus told her that Mary had "chosen the better thing." She had noticed when Jesus came into the room, and nothing else mattered except for Him. Later, in John 11, after their brother Lazarus had died, a strange thing happened. Martha said to Jesus, "Lord, if you would have been here, my brother would not have died." Jesus proceeded to ask her if she believed and reminded her of who He was. A few moments later, Mary came and made the exact same statement: "Lord, if you would have been here, my brother would not have died." She says this while weeping at His feet, and her heart was exposed. So Mary didn't get a reminder, she got an answer! Instead of asking her about her faith, Jesus asked Mary a question: "Where have you laid him?" He had resurrection on His mind! Mary didn't get a reminder, because she didn't need one. When the Lord comes down, He will always call you up. That day, He called Lazarus up from the grave, and Mary heard him coming.

> *And all the people saw the thunderings, and the lightnings, and the noise of the trumpet, and the mountain smoking: and when the people saw it, they removed, and stood afar off. And they said unto Moses, Speak thou with us, and we will hear: but let not God speak with us, lest we die. And Moses said unto the people, Fear not: for God is come to prove you, and that his fear may be before your faces, that ye sin not. And the people stood afar off, and Moses drew near unto the thick darkness where God was* (Exodus 20:18–21).

The people deliberately chose to be "afar off." This was the position that Peter took just before he denied the Lord, after Judas had betrayed Jesus. This is the position many of the disciples took, according to the gospels, while Jesus was walking toward Calvary. It is a position that is very hard to recover from, for we often find comfort there. When you are walking afar off, you don't notice the little things, the things of pain and requirement. You are afar off, and not much hurts you. But at the same time, you cannot see the glorious things, either, because you are too far away.

Israelites had made their choice: they decided to be a people who willingly walked "afar off" from God. But Moses had chosen "a better thing." When we are sanctified in Him, He is the only one that matters. We can see nothing else because all the torments and afflictions hidden deep in our soul have been captured by God.

It's one thing to know He came down, another to hear Him say, "Come up!" and still another to go up when you are called. "Going up" costs something. To "go up" we have to leave our baggage behind, because we will never make the trip carrying all that weight. Will you "go up," or have another do it for you? Will you draw near like Moses, or walk afar off like the Israelites?

Do you think that you are not worthy or able to "go up" to the mountain of God? Listen, you may think there are several reasons why you don't qualify to "come on up," but try to beat these:

David's armor didn't fit. Mark was rejected by Paul. Timothy had ulcers. Hosea's wife was a prostitute. Amos's only training was in the school of fig tree pruning. Jacob was a liar. David had an affair. Solomon was too rich. Abraham was too old. Josiah was too young. Peter was afraid of death. Lazarus was dead. John was self-righteous. Job had fear and a nag for a wife. Naomi was a widow. Gideon was a nobody. Jeremiah was depressed and suicidal. Elijah was burned-out. John the Baptist was a loudmouth. Martha was a worrywart. Samson had long hair. Noah got drunk. Elisha had a short fuse, so did Paul, and so do I. Maybe you do, too!

But God announced that it was time for all of them to "come on up"—and your name is included in the invitation!

The funny thing about "The Mountain of God" is that it never goes away. The Israelites chose to stay on the other side, a short distance away from where Moses was. They made the decision in their hearts, and that decision was manifested when God told them to stay at the base of the mountain. Clearly, they had not prepared and couldn't trust. Moses wasn't going to let who Israel was get in his way or define him. They could have drawn closer, as Moses did, but they had no desire to. They could have had a burning bush experience like Moses did, but they turned away from that and chose another path.

So, the peoples' choice had been made, and the work of Moses was almost complete. They captured their identity from their surroundings and not their destiny in God. Wrapping yourself around the wrong identity, based upon perceived reality, can be fatal. That identity did not include a mountain; it would only include a few, very small hills and a vast wasteland of wilderness. Not very glorious, but that's what they had chosen. When we are full of ourselves, we cannot handle the fullness of God, and we disqualify ourselves from climbing His mountain.

Sometimes we get so tired of the fight that we just give up and give in. We can convince ourselves that all of our effort is not necessary and allow ourselves to be seduced and lulled into a state of bland neutrality. Surely by now you have come to understand that to go forward and take the mountain that looms in front of you, you have to not only lose the baggage that you've been carrying around, but you also have to choose and commit to take that mountain.

CHAPTER 22

Sabbath Moments

See, for that the Lord hath given you the sabbath, there-fore he giveth you on the sixth day the bread of two days; abide ye every man in his place, let no man go out of his place on the seventh day. So the people rested on the seventh day (Exodus 16:29–30).

The Lord spent time instructing the people about the way it was going to be. When we are left to our own devices, often we forget the important things because we are so busy focusing on the "urgent" things. If we are only focusing on the urgent things of life, we will never be able to go past relationship and get into fellowship. We will be stuck in the mode of a spiritual fireman, continually putting out fires and never simply enjoying who God is. The Lord has both physical and spiritual reasons why He wants His people to rest one day a week. Our bodies need that rest, and our spirits need time to soar with Christ. To truly understand the Sabbath as a lifestyle, let us take it a step further and bring the Sabbath into an abiding attitude.

If thou turn away thy foot from the sabbath, from doing thy pleasure on my holy day; and call the sabbath a delight, the holy of the Lord, honourable; and shalt honour him, not doing thine own ways, nor finding thine own pleasure, nor speaking thine own words: Then shalt thou delight thyself in the Lord; and I will cause thee to ride upon the high places of the earth, and feed thee with the heritage of Jacob thy father: for the mouth of the Lord hath spoken it (Isaiah 58:13–14).

Remember the sabbath day, to keep it holy (Exodus 20:8).

The *Merriam-Webster Dictionary* defines "Sabbath" as a "time of rest," while *Strong's* calls it an "intermission" (*shabbath*, #H7676). So "Sabbath" is a "restful intermission." We should do that every day! Taking a Sabbath every day means that you are going to reflect on not only what God is doing in you, but what He wants to do in you that day. Taking a Sabbath is to ensure that your day doesn't start commanding and confusing you; it's ensuring that the fruit of the Spirit is alive and well in you. When you take a daily Sabbath, you are taking a moment to collect yourself and separate yourself from what's going on around you. This is not to say that you should forsake the coming together with your brethren on a scheduled day in a house of worship. In fact, if you take daily Sabbaths, you will enjoy those weekly Sabbath times together even more, because you will be more settled and able to be a blessing to others. When you take a daily Sabbath, you are seeking wisdom, rest and direction.

David should have taken a Sabbath when he saw Bathsheba. Samson should have taken a Sabbath when he saw Delilah. Adam should have taken a Sabbath when he saw that fruit in the hand of his wife. Jonah should have taken a Sabbath before he jumped on the boat. Abraham should have taken a Sabbath when Sarah shoved him into Hagar's tent. Peter should have taken a Sabbath before he grabbed a sword, and Judas should have taken a Sabbath before he entertained evil.

What we have just read is that if we call the "Sabbath a delight...then we will ride on the high places of the earth and be fed with the heritage of Jacob." The heritage of Jacob was one of the most abundant places of favor a man could walk in. In spite of his earlier error, once Jacob repented, he was blessed beyond measure with promises that would last for generations. If there was redemption for Jacob's lying, scheming soul, then surely there is hope for us!

If we do not rest in God, we will suffer from unbelief.

While we have learned that "Sabbath" means a restful intermission, "delight," in the context of this scripture, indicates it should be a time of priority. Our moments of resting in and leaning on Jesus in the midst of our day need to be a time of priority. Reading, worship and prayer create a life with a strong spiritual foundation; but a life that takes Sabbath moments regularly, in addition to those things, has a joy in their foundation. If we cannot rest in the Lord and be still and quiet before Him, we will not be able to delight ourselves in Him. If we cannot delight ourselves in Him, we will not be able to trust Him. Delighting in the Lord is to put Him first and walk in knowing Him and not just knowing of Him.

> For he that is entered into his rest, he also hath ceased from his own works, as God did from his. Let us labour therefore to enter into that rest, lest any man fall after the same example of unbelief (Hebrews 4:10–11).

If we do not rest in God, we will suffer from unbelief. And if we don't believe God, we can't trust Him, and our faith will remain weak.

The Lord gave the Israelite nation rules, guidelines and laws by which to live. He set up an almost military strategy for their success. He gave them a beautiful picture of how it would be if they would obey, and reminded them of the tragedy of disobedience. God told them about the angels, and even how to deal with this mighty force and resource that He had created. God told them that He would drive out the inhabitants of the land where they were going, and He would do it little by little, so they could learn to trust Him, and so that the land wouldn't be too much work for them. God had a perfect plan, but it was given to a people who were bound by the desire for imperfection. Moses had learned to rest in God; Israel was still wrestling.

Meeting with God

> *And the glory of the Lord abode upon mount Sinai, and the cloud covered it in six days: and the seventh day he called unto Moses out of the midst of the cloud. And the sight of the glory of the Lord was like devouring fire on the top of the mount in the eyes of the children of Israel. And Moses went into the midst of the cloud, and gat him up into the mount: and Moses was in the mount forty days and forty nights* (Exodus 24:16–18).

Moses stood on top of this flaming mountain covered in a cloud, and the Israelites saw it. Moses then disappeared into the midst of the cloud. That sight alone should have kept them going for 40 days, but it didn't.

Moses met God one-on-one that day, and continued meeting with Him for almost six weeks. Moses knew what this was like; he could remember the burning bush in Midian. He would not argue with the presence of God this time; he would walk into it. This was Israel's chance to have a burning experience with God. A mountain on fire that would surely consume their lusts and desires. But alas, they chose the backside of the desert, the place where trust could never be found. But Moses ran toward the voice of his Maker.

On the mountain, the Lord God Almighty proceeded to tell Moses about first fruit offerings, blessings, cursings, Sabbaths, tabernacles, materials and men that He had ordained and equipped to accomplish great things in the camp and in the building of the Lord's house in the wilderness. He had a 40-day conversation with Moses. And in the end, Moses walked away with a miraculous declaration of God's mandate for blessing: the Ten Commandments on stone, written by the very finger of God.

And he gave unto Moses, when he had made an end of communing with him upon mount Sinai, two tables of testimony, tables of stone, written with the finger of God (Exodus 31:18).

The People Longed for Egypt

Then it happened: The people got bored while Moses was on the mountain. Earlier in scripture, in Exodus 24, when Moses was going up to Mount Sinai, all the men that God gave to Moses saw God, "and there was under his feet as it were a paved work of sapphire stone, and as it were the body of heaven in his clearness...." They saw God and ate and drank (all except for Moses and Joshua). They made God and His presence common, and because of it, they attempted to mix Him up with what they were doing.

Aaron, Hur, Nadab, Abihu and 70 of the elders were told to stay at the base of the mountain after they saw God, and they were told to manage things for 40 days while Moses and Joshua went up further. They were instructed to mediate any disputes and keep track of things.

While the very finger of God was carving through stone on a mountain filled with smoke and fire above their heads, His children decided that building an altar to a false god of Egypt would be a good idea. They still longed for Egypt. They tarried with it in their hearts until their desire overcame who the Lord had asked them to become. Where were the ministers that Moses put in charge? Who knows?

Aaron eventually showed up to give them instructions on how to properly turn this idol into a false god, and he began to carve it with his own priestly hands. In chapter 23, God told the people (and was very specific when He did), "Don't make any graven images!" They had only been out of Egypt less than a year at this point. The Red Sea had parted behind them as a fantastic display of God's power and provision, but a people who are only temporarily convinced and forever uncommitted will never suffer to know their God or truly experience Him.

And when the people saw that Moses delayed to come down...they rose up early on the morrow, and offered burnt offerings, and brought peace offerings [to the false god they had created in the shape of a calf]; and the people sat down to eat and to drink, and rose up to play (Exodus 32).

I wonder, was this the same kind of "eating and drinking" some of them did earlier at the base of Mount Sinai, when God was revealing Himself to them there? You know, when they actually saw Him? We must never confuse holiness with foolishness!

The Word says, "They rose up to play." Had being entertained become so important to the people? Had being in control become everything? They couldn't wait on God because they didn't trust Him. They said that Moses was "delayed," but the truth was, he was right on time. It was the people who had not bothered to ask God what time it was. Has your need for entertainment become your occupation while you are waiting on Jesus? The attitudes of those we surround ourselves with will become our attitudes before too long.

The enemy loves to make it appear that God has forsaken us. He loves to give us a cause that doesn't belong to Christ. These people were wearing earrings of gold, even their sons were, which was a powerful indicator of Egyptian dress. This fact is mentioned for a reason. They were looking like Egyptians and acting like Egyptians. They made an Egyptian idol, and their leader announced that it was now their god. They worshipped it and played. Their need for comfort went too far this time.

And they [the Israelites] made a calf in those days, and offered sacrifice unto the idol, and rejoiced in the works of their own hands (Acts 7:41).

When they were "rejoicing in the works of their own hands," they were worshipping themselves. We can only come into communion and agreement with the one we are willing to worship! When we don't agree with God, we eliminate the favor of God from our lives.

We cannot agree with God and ourselves at the same time because God doesn't share His worship with anyone. We must choose who is right and worthy—God or us!

> *And the Lord said unto Moses, Go, get thee down; for thy people, which thou broughtest out of the land of Egypt, have corrupted themselves....And the Lord said unto Moses, I have seen this people, and, behold, it is a stiffnecked people: Now therefore let me alone, that my wrath may wax hot against them, and that I may consume them: and I will make of thee a great nation. And Moses besought the Lord his God [for the people].... And when Joshua heard the noise of the people as they shouted, he said unto Moses, There is a noise of war in the camp....And Moses said unto Aaron, What did this people unto thee, that thou hast brought so great a sin upon them? And Aaron said,...I said unto them, Whosoever hath any gold, let them break it off. So they gave it me: then I cast it into the fire, and there came out this calf* (Exodus 32:7, 9-10, 17, 21, 24).

Right, the calf just "came out"! The people corrupted themselves by worshipping a false god, which they created in the shape of a calf. God declared that He had had it with this "stiffnecked" people, and He was going to wipe them out and just make a great nation out of Moses. No doubt, that looked like a pretty good offer to Moses—no more whining, griping people to deal with. Even as a vessel, it was probably tempting just to end the battle with an unwilling people because Moses, himself, was willing to do it correctly. But as a friend of God, he only had one option, and that was to defend the honor of God, even to God Himself. When God "repents" of the thought of wiping the people out in Exodus 32:14, what that means is that God comforted Himself, took a breath and felt sorry for the people. God called these people "the people of Moses." That was an honor because it meant that God had shared His vision with Moses—not His identity, but His vision.

The Sounds of War

Joshua, the man who would not leave the tabernacle, the man who was willing to do anything to be in the presence of the Lord, was being taught by God Himself to hear the sound of war. God taught Joshua to hear the sound of spiritual war, since he would be a man of many battles in the future. If we are able to hear it in the spirit, we shall be able to overcome it in the flesh! Oh, that we would finally understand that and forever operate in it. Joshua heard the sound of war as the people were singing and shouting down below them. When Moses finally ventured down the mountain, Joshua was watching and learning as they saw the horrifying sight of the people running around naked, dancing and singing before a golden calf that they called a god.

Moses was overcome with righteous indignation. The question is, was Moses acting out of his own anger, or God's? We have to believe that this day, it was God's. Still, a Sabbath moment could have saved some priceless pieces of artwork drawn by God's own hand.

Moses threw the tablets of the Ten Commandments down and they broke. He took the calf, burnt it up and pounded it into the ground until it was powder, and then he threw the powder into some water and made the people drink it. Then he went after Aaron and chewed him out. Moses stood at the entrance of the camp and asked, "Who is on the Lord's side?" The Levites answered the question by moving from where they were and stood next to Moses. There was a civil war that day because people got confused and bored. They forgot their cause and the One who gave them that cause. That day, 300,000 people were killed because of compromise and a lack of commitment.

Moses then went to God and repented for the people and asked God to bless them. Moses echoed God's own heart back to Him; that's how we know he had truly made it into the land of friendship. God's desires were finally more important than his own. Moses begged for the people and went so far as to say he'd be willing to take their place and be blotted out, as long as they could still be called the people of God and be worthy of a blessing. Moses knew that it was God's desire to bless His children; that is always God's desire. The Lord told Moses to go to the place He was leading them, and He sent an angel to guide the way.

Moses went back around the mountain and took time to be alone with God. When he took a Sabbath moment, he heard God. In the confusion and chaos that was going on around him, eventually, he found a Sabbath moment and became better for it. So many times if we would have just taken time, a tragedy would not have happened. If we would have just settled down in that moment, we would not have said things we later regretted or done things that couldn't be undone.

Jesus was good at taking these Sabbath moments. He often went away alone to visit with His Father or ponder the things that were happening. After His cousin, John the Baptist, was beheaded, we see Him going for a Sabbath moment to be alone. We see Him going there often. Maybe if we found those moments more frequently, the fruit of the Spirit in our lives wouldn't be so hidden. When we are alone with God, gaining His wisdom and patience, we aren't so provoked to react to the seemingly urgent things around us. Then we have more opportunity and energy to respond to actual emergencies.

It doesn't take a long time, and it doesn't cost any money to have a Sabbath moment. In those times when we are not only coming to hear God, but are planning on hearing Him, the sounds are so clear and pure. It's a wonderful thing to be in the middle of a Sabbath moment and not feel the push of circumstances around you.

CHAPTER 23

Face-to-Face Worship

And the Lord spoke to Moses face to face, as a man spea-keth unto his friend.... And [Moses] said unto him, If thy presence go not with me, carry us not up hence.... I beseech thee, shew me thy glory. And he said, I will make all my goodness pass before thee, and I will proclaim the name of the Lord before thee; and will be gracious to whom I will be gracious, and will shew mercy on whom I will shew mercy (Exodus 33: 11, 15, 18-19).

Face-to-face is heart to heart. Heart to heart is friendship. The Lord was speaking to Moses as a friend now. Always re-member, the Lord is not intimate with those He is dating, only those who are married to Him. In Exodus 33, "friend" (*rea,* #H7453) literally means "companion...husband, lover," or, in other words, spouse. Face-to-face fellowship is only found in a marriage relationship with the Lord, the kind of relationship that moves in fellowship, partnership and communion.

In verse 15, Moses made a statement that paralleled an earlier day. At the burning bush, when he wouldn't go with God, no matter what God did, because His presence wasn't enough, Moses insist-ed on another way, and God gave him Aaron. When we refuse to pay the price for friendship, we usually gravitate toward a cheap substitute to cover our lack. But after Moses became a vessel and landed in the place of friendship, he didn't need a crutch anymore. His wounds were healed, and he was a man looking for his Friend. He said, "If thy presence go not with me, carry us not up hence." In essence he was saying, "Lord, if You don't go with me, I don't want to go. I just want You." He's not talking about stuttering, worrying about people's words, or acting out fear or rejection here—he just wants the Lord to be with him. *Moses didn't need any more excuses because he had finally recovered from himself.*

Moses was not seeking power; he had seen plenty of that, by now he was "the miracle man." What he truly wanted went past power: it was presence. He wanted to see God's person, not His power. He was seeking who God is, not what God can do. He had already seen what God can do, probably more than anyone; and he determined that, although he had witnessed great things, he just wanted God. He wanted to know his Friend and walk in His presence more than anything.

Finding Grace

Finding grace is to live in inherited authority. Moses came to understand what grace is. It isn't mercy. He needed mercy as a man more than anything. Although he enjoyed the mercy of God, he still needed the grace. He craved it; for it is the inherited right of a saint to walk in the authority of God Himself. We do this through Jesus Christ, as children of our heavenly Father. Moses did it through friendship.

Jesus said that He is the friend who sticks closer than a brother, and that if we obey Him, He calls us friends and not servants. When the Lord told Paul in 2 Corinthians 12:9, "My grace is sufficient for thee: for my strength is made perfect in weakness," Paul understood that the Lord was saying His grace was all he needed. Because Paul acknowledged that he couldn't do it without the Lord, it made the Lord's strength in him perfect. The word "grace" here, when it is studied out, indicates it is an inherited right or ability. When Peter said to "grow in grace," he was saying to walk in your inheritance. He didn't mean we needed to grow in mercy, or something that someone could hand to us. So, the Lord was telling Paul, "Your inheritance is sufficient for you; I will make you strong." Paul was able to finish the verse gladly with this comment, "Most gladly therefore will I rather glory in my infirmities, that the power of Christ may rest upon me." He wasn't saying that he wanted infirmities; he was saying they didn't matter. All that mattered was Christ, and he could participate in that because he was a man with an inheritance.

When I read the word "grace" in the Word of God, I often think of it as "inheritance." In fact, when I was very ill and trying to be brave, I'd read that scripture, "His grace is sufficient for me," and would feel like I was being held hostage by my pain. I thought, "I just have to wait. What is going on is sufficient, and that's that!" But when the Lord showed me what grace really was, that verse ignited me. "My inherited right—all my abilities in Jesus Christ—will make me able to overcome this trial. I have Calvary on my side and the fruit of the Spirit within me. No matter how bad I feel, I have an inherited right to overcome whatever is going on, so I will! I am more than a conqueror in Him, and Jesus said that I should be happy because He already overcame this world." That's a different way of looking at that verse, and it helped! The Lord is counting on us evolving from servanthood to friendship, to enjoy His fullness and walk in His authority to abide in the land of His grace.

God's Goodness
When Moses asked to see the glory of God, he was asking to see His goodness. How often we underrate the sheer joy of the goodness of God. His goodness was never more on display than at Calvary. It was never more perfect than at that point and is still multiplying upon us every time we engage in a thought of Calvary. Matthew 6:33 says to "Seek ye first the kingdom of God, and his righteousness; and all these things shall be added unto you." Whatever we need in life are "all these things," but for today, let us ponder how the Kingdom work and the goodness of a risen Savior affects our lives. When we truly understand the "goodness" of Calvary, it so overwhelms us that we can barely stand up under it. It is a speechless moment in time, full of glory and power.

Too often, we want to see something with our physical eyes: the glorious, the glitter, the gold dust. Although God can be in those things, when we search for those things wanting power rather than

Christ, the enemy can, just as the magicians did, produce an imitation by a false spirit. God is all about the miraculous; He rides upon the mysterious wonder of His acts upon the earth. But He is evermore the God of the "still, small voice," as He was for Elijah. If we are seeking Him and not His power, then we shall find all the power that is held within who He is. We have a relationship with Jesus Christ through the Holy Spirit; we don't have a relationship with His power. And if we walk closely with Him, that relationship will turn into a face-to-face fellowship as we learn to trust Him. We were meant to have that kind of fellowship with our God. We were made for it, way back in the Garden of Eden.

Moses asked to see the goodness or very character of God, and he was not disappointed. The Lord was going to cause His glory, or His goodness, to pass by Moses; and it was so pure, so absolutely amazing, that the human heart and mind, eye and soul would perish at the sight of it. Therefore, God covered Moses with His hand as he rested in the cleft of a rock, and the communion of the ages commenced. Moses would never be the same after he embraced this friendship of face-to-face fellowship, walking in the glory of God. When you have been exposed to the true nature and character of God, it changes you.

There is something irresistible about the perfection of God. Moses had tasted of it, and now he would never be the same; he would crave it all the days of his life.

> *And be ready in the morning, and come up in the morning unto mount Sinai, and present thyself there to me in the top of the mount* (Exodus 34:2).

The Lord was going to give Moses another set of the Ten Commandments and asked Moses to come to the top of Mount Sinai again. But look how God did it. He gave Moses instructions on how to walk in His glory:

1. Be ready.
2. Come up.
3. Present yourself!

These are instructions for life. How can we get ready? By being prepared to meet the Lord (finding ways to be full of Him). How can we come up? By stopping our world as Mary did and Moses does here (taking "Sabbath moments" when the Holy Spirit petitions you to, throughout the day). And how do we present ourselves? By being willing and obedient (trusting God to take care of us, no matter what).

Moses Worshipped God

Once Moses followed these instructions, he did something that we have never seen him do before—he worshipped God! Exodus 34:8 records this of Moses after he experienced the glory of God: "And Moses made haste and bowed his head toward the earth and he worshipped." In the Hebrew text, this word "worshipped" (*shachah*, #H7812), as used here, literally means to "prostrate (especially reflexive, in homage to royalty or God)...obeisance, do reverence." He was not singing, praying or talking; he was worshipping! Praise is about what God can do. Worship is about who God is. Praise talks about what is going on down here; God inhabits that. But true worship is about what is going on in heaven. The Psalms mention praise 188 times, but worship is only mentioned 14 times.

True worship is found only in a moment of selflessness. It is a reckless abandon to who God is, not what He is doing. True worship needs nothing; it wants nothing. It will pray the heart of God back to God in adoration of who He is. It is the most powerful thing a creation can do; it is a prayer from the depths of who we are. It is not a song or an action; it is an undoing of flesh and soul to Him. You can live your life to praise God, but worshipping Him is something that will make you stop whatever you are doing.

True worship is to allow your heart
to speak the words of your soul.

It was when Gideon worshipped that he realized who God was calling him to be; he understood his identity. When Job worshipped, he remembered what was real and not what was realized. When David worshipped, he knew the forgiveness and protection of God. Only through worship can we walk in the glory. When we are worshipping, we are seeking His heart; not what He can do, but who He is. Much of what God does springs from who He is. But when we seek one without the other, we shall not be called the friends of God. True worship is to take that Sabbath moment and be still before Him. True worship is to allow your heart to speak the words of your soul. When Moses worshipped, he was "paying homage to and reverencing royalty."

God loves to give us second chances, and He does that here with the Israelites in Exodus 34. He brought Moses back up the mountain again for one more 40-day tour and gave him another set of Ten Commandments. When Moses came down off the mountain this time, the Israelites saw the face of a man who was in the middle of a divine friendship.

> *And it came to pass, when Moses came down from Mount Sinai with the two tables of testimony in Moses' hand, when he came down from the mount, that Moses wist not that the skin of his face shone while he talked with him.... And till Moses had done speaking with them, he put a vail on his face. But when Moses went in before the Lord to speak with him, he took the vail off, until he came out* (Exodus 34:29–34).

Here is a man who had nothing left to lose. It was all gone; God alone remained. When you have seen God's glory, it changes you. When Jesus Christ lives inside you, it is supposed to change you. People are supposed to notice, and if they don't, then your walk with the Lord isn't all that glorious, and that's a shame. The glory had overcome Moses, and it showed.

Moses had to wear a veil over his face because the people weren't prepared to see the glory of God; they weren't ready. God comes where preparation has been made. When Daniel saw the vision that nobody around him did, they fainted because they weren't prepared. When Jesus raised Jairus's daughter from the dead, He had to send people out of the room because they were not prepared to see it. Often when the Lord healed somebody, He said, "Go, and don't tell anyone just yet." Why? They weren't ready to know Him. Gehazi couldn't raise the Shuhamite's son from the dead; he wasn't Elisha. Elisha was ready, but Gehazi wasn't. Mary of Bethany was ready to receive a miracle, but Martha wasn't.

Are you ready? Perhaps you have had trouble making up your mind as you consider venturing out into the land of fellowship. Let me tell you a story I heard from a man named Jess, who attended a meeting I conducted in San Jose, California, and let's see if he can't convince you that there is no time like the present to welcome, engage and abide in a deeper walk with Christ:

Walking Close to God

Jess has a nice little family on the west side of San Francisco. Jess had attended a crusade and decided that he would live a life that would be more concerned about others than himself. He heard a sermon about the Good Samaritan and was desperate to physically express the commitment that he made during the church service. Jess was typically a selfish man, and he admitted it. However, he was changed that day and longed to live out the life of the Good Samaritan. He went to work as usual, but left early to run errands. He passed by an alley on the way to the parking garage and heard yelling and shouting. He ignored it, because that's what he had trained himself to do all those years, so it came naturally to him. He continued walking. The yelling turned into screaming. He kept walking. It was probably a gang fight or a lover's spat; he couldn't decide which and didn't care. But his steps became heavier as the Holy Spirit reminded him of the Samaritan and the elements of Christ in the man.

Finally, Jess stopped in his tracks. Everything became clear to him. He knew he had to retrace his steps and offer help, even at the expense of his own life. He had always known himself to be a passive coward before, and he was surprised at the speed with which he ran back to the alley. When the Holy Spirit gets ahold of a determined mind, it's all supernatural from there.

Jess came upon the alley and yelled forcefully, "What's going on in here?" Three men stood up and angrily glared at him. Slowly, they walked toward him. Then they stopped. Jess said, "You boys better leave now, don't you think?" They nodded and passed by him quickly, turning onto the street. Jess hurried to the back of the alley, wondering who was slumped in a ball, hiding in the corner of this dirty alley. He approached the figure and knelt down, as if he was living the life of the Good Samaritan in the 21st century. He said, "Are you okay? I have come to help you; I won't hurt you." The girl lifted up her head in the dark alley and said through her sobbing, "Oh, thank you, Daddy!" It was his daughter, Maryanne! She had been going to his office to give him a surprise visit, not knowing he had left early that day. She was abducted along the way and dragged down the alley just moments before he was passing by. Thankfully, she was completely unharmed.

The day that Jess decided to come into agreement with God, favor flowed in abundance. For a brief moment, Jess had dared to believe that God knew what He was doing. When the Lord said, "Come on up," he said, "I'm coming right now!" When the Lord said, "Face-to-face fellowship is going to cost you some of yourself," he said, "Great idea." When the Lord said, "Walk in My grace and do what I would do," he said, "Just show me how!" He believed the results were everlasting and that they mattered. He was right.

I guess doing the right thing just because it's right is one of the things that comes automatically after a while. When we've become accustomed to the sound of the Lord's voice, because we choose to abide in those Sabbath moments and worship, then finding our way back there isn't hard; it's a natural act. May we be found in the midst of worship easily and effectively to glorify the Lord each and every day.

CHAPTER 24

The Promise of Canaan

He made known his ways unto Moses, his acts unto the children of Israel (Psalm 103:7).

M oses suffered to live that statement out. When you reach for fellowship as Moses did, you are reaching for the truth of who God is. You are no longer content knowing what He does; you now must know the heart of the reason behind it. When you give God everything, He can do anything. Years ago that was a scary thought to Moses, but today he takes comfort in it.

The first president of the United States, General George Washington, is credited with saying, "It is not sufficient for a man to be a passing friend or a well-wisher to the cause." And so it is with God. He is not interested in entering into fellowship with a "fair-weather friend." They will maintain a relationship, but God desires one who will look at Him no matter what the circumstances are and say, "I came for You, not for what You can do, but because of who You are!" What God does is part of who He is, but when that's all we know and all we seek, we will forever have His hand and never see His face. One is good; the other is better. One will shout, "My love is contingent on what I get from You." The other will shout, "No matter what comes my way, Jesus is enough!"

The name "Canaan," in my studies, indicated that it was a land meant to be conquered (see *kana*, #H3665). But it must be a land remembered and desired before it can be conquered. The Israelites could not accept this challenge; they complained almost nonstop and talked themselves out of their promises. They announced to God that they wished they were dead or, at least, back in bondage in Egypt. Throughout their tenure upon the earth, they tried to emotionally destroy Moses. They called him names, started rumors about him and even tried to kill him. They complained that they missed the food and comfortable routine of Egypt. (Comfort? They were slaves who were beaten!) They were supernaturally fed manna from heaven and had quail stacked up four feet high a day's journey on either side of them. But it was not enough! His family and most of his leaders, along with all the people, came against Moses, and this horror continued for 40 years.

Because they refused to walk in the power and authority of being heirs, they frustrated the plan of God. What we shout in a time of trial reveals what God will honor and what He won't.

We will skip much of the indiscretion of the Israelites and all the times they forsook God and refused to trust Him. They adamantly stated over and over again that they didn't want what God wanted, and they refused to trust Him, even when they were looking at the Canaan county line. They tasted the fruit of the land and saw the abundance of it. They tasted the pomegranates and declared them "not good enough." They would later cry for the pomegranates of Egypt because that's where their hearts were. They refused to change their desires; they insisted on keeping their old flesh, the flesh that refused to walk in redemption. God's provision was not enough, because it came with a cost—the cost of trusting God.

The Israelites could not grasp the reality of what was important to God: Canaan was a destination, not an occupation. Canaan was where they were going, not who they were becoming. Canaan was an object of trust, but not the main ingredient of trust. The journey was never about getting to Canaan; it was all about getting to God!

The giants were merely a force
that existed to fuel the arrival of the glory of God.

They had not seen a giant, but they had seen the good fruit of the land. What they had never seen was a greater threat to them than the power of what they had seen. They were overwhelmed by the thought of having to pay a price in battle. Peace is often the product of a war. To maintain and enjoy peace, often we must fight to keep it. It is the great temptation of mankind to settle into a comfortable chair as life waltzes by in order to avoid the battle. What the people didn't understand was a basic rule of warfare: with big promises, often there is a big adversary. There is a reason why promises rarely look like reality until they get here—it builds trust! The giants were merely a force that existed to fuel the arrival of the deliverance and glory of God, but the Israelites couldn't trust God for that.

When we are in the doorway of God's promise, we need to be careful lest our fear and complaining blind us; because blindness leads to failure. Spiritual blindness will cause us to have horizontal vision and be able to only see those things that surround us. To be a people of promise who can trust, we must be vertical visionaries, seeing the things that are above us, and even calling out that which is not (down here) as if it were (because it is up there). If you cannot trust, having vertical vision is almost impossible. Moses was a vertical man leading a horizontal people in a crisscrossed world. Moses understood the statement, "Whatever you hold to be true is binding upon you!" He believed it and was willing to live his life to prove it.

They were told that the enemy was their bread. The enemy was going to be the fuel that brought the honor to God, as God brought the deliverance. But the prospect of suffering caused this people to crave failure and run to compromise, which forbade God from giving them the promise that He longed to give them.

Moses sent 12 men into Canaan to "spy out the land." They stayed for 40 days and came back with food so abundant that it was astonishing to everyone. The people were told, "Surely this is a land that flows with milk and honey, just as God told us!" Two men were ready to go and take the land right then. Ten said, "We should stop a minute and talk about how big the giants are over there." That was enough to start the fatal mutinous revolt. Big grapes had big giants that planted them in God's big country. But it was still

God's country, and He would give it to whomever He chose. They had not understood then, nor would they ever understand, that big promises have big adversaries. And further, they never hooked up with the reality that their God was even bigger than the giants. Although our promises have big adversaries, they have an even bigger advocate! The lack of that knowledge would cost them everything this time. The two men, Joshua and Caleb, stood to proclaim truth, but nobody was listening except Moses, and the people wouldn't let his vote count!

We shall leave the Israelites where we found them, for they really haven't moved forward much at all. The scenery may have been different, but their hearts still had not found God. They were continually acting like a people without a vision or goal. After a while, what you complain about is what you become, and they would get to live that truth out. They were wandering around as God's children, with His name upon them, yet still hadn't understood "they are not their own, they have been bought with a price." Luke 12:48 has always been true, from the beginning of time until today: "To whom much is given, much is required."

We cannot say we believe something and then allow our actions and words to shout the opposite, because the presence and power of God demands a proper response.

Their complaining finally caught up with their destiny and changed it! There would be no Canaan for these people after all. Earlier, God called Moses to lead the people out of Egypt and into Canaan. Now, God is telling Moses to lead them away from Canaan and into the wilderness so they would be sure to have enough to complain about, since that was where their hearts seemed to be. Yesterday, Moses was their leader, today he would become their shepherd: the one who would be willing to suffer with them simply because God had asked him to.

Moses Became Their Shepherd

As they headed into the wilderness and walked away from the promised land, the people needed a shepherd. And guess who it was? Moses, the friend of God! Moses didn't say, "Wait a minute,

I didn't do anything wrong!" He simply submitted, because that's who he was now. He trusted God, not for the promise, but for the hope of friendship that lay within that promise. The hope of continuing his friendship with his God propelled him into the wilderness with this rebellious people. As long as God was going with him, he didn't seem to care where he was headed. When God told Moses to make a U-turn, he didn't even flinch. "Tomorrow turn you and get you into the wilderness by the way of the Red Sea." So close, but yet so far away was this land of Canaan, but their friendship just kept getting closer and closer.

This was a completely different man than the one who was trying to find a reason to stay in Midian when the bush was burning. This was a man who had been captured by the heart of God and had been provoked to "go further." This man, Moses, was not concerned about himself anymore, but only about the concerns of his Maker and Friend, his God.

The wilderness experience is full of one uprising after another. The books of Numbers and Deuteronomy are full of the exploits of these people who refused to trust God. The stories of glory are written down as God delivers one miracle after another, one form of justice and love after another. All the while His friend, Moses, looks on with a long-suffering eye.

They were ushered away from Canaan into the wilderness because of their mistrust and disbelief while eating grapes and hearing about giants. Moses took the punishment along with the people because his willingness to be God's friend made him able to do so. Moses trusted God even in this. His reward would be greater than he could have ever imagined. Moses would walk in an honor that would last through the timeless ages of eternity because he brought endless glory to God. The name of Moses lingers throughout history as the trademark of face-to-face fellowship.

Moses began to instruct the people to go back into the wilderness and sent messengers to find a safe road to travel. None of the inhabitants of the surrounding lands looked upon the Israelites with either favor or fear. They would not give them a safe crossing without a fight, and Israel was not in any shape to fight. There was a day when the Israelites evoked fear in the people around them. Often, they were given favor because of that fear. But those days were long gone. Israel had become a laughingstock among their neighbors because of their rebellious, selfish hearts. They were nomads—wanderers who had to beg to cross the land that they should have owned. This was the land they refused to fight for, even after the God who parted the Red Sea had secured it for them as a gift. And now, they had to beg just to touch it. Years before, all of Egypt shook as the people left because of the power of God that went before them. The world stood in awe of this God who was calling a people out to Himself. That was back when it mattered to them. Now, they were disobedient. So they would lose the land; and they knew it.

> *Then came the children of Israel, even the whole congregation, into the desert of Zin in the first month: and the people abode in Kadesh; and Miriam died there, and was buried there. And there was no water for the congregation: and they gathered themselves together against Moses and against Aaron. And the people chode with Moses, and spake, saying, Would God that we had died when our brethren died before the Lord! And why have ye brought up the congregation of the Lord into this wilderness, that we and our cattle should die there? And wherefore have ye made us to come up out of Egypt, to bring us in unto this evil place? it is no place of seed, or of figs, or of vines, or of pomegranates; neither is there any water to drink.*

> *And Moses and Aaron went from the presence of the assembly unto the door of the tabernacle of the congregation, and they fell upon their faces: and the glory of the Lord appeared unto them. And the Lord spake unto Moses, saying, Take the rod, and gather thou the assembly together, thou, and Aaron thy brother, and speak ye unto the rock before their eyes; and it shall give forth his water, and thou shalt bring forth to them water out of the rock:*

so thou shalt give the congregation and their beasts drink. And Moses took the rod from before the Lord, as he commanded him. And Moses and Aaron gathered the congregation together before the rock, and he said unto them, Hear now, ye rebels; must we fetch you water out of this rock? And Moses lifted up his hand, and with his rod he smote the rock twice: and the water came out abundantly, and the congregation drank, and their beasts also.

And the Lord spake unto Moses and Aaron, Because ye believed me not, to sanctify me in the eyes of the children of Israel, therefore ye shall not bring this congregation into the land which I have given them. This is the water of Meribah; because the children of Israel strove with the Lord, and he was sanctified in them…. And Moses did as the Lord commanded: and they went up into mount Hor in the sight of all the congregation (Numbers 20:1–13, 27).

A Moment of Indiscretion

It was the year that Miriam died. Moses was spent, exhausted and emotional. He should have taken a time-out. He should have sat in the Sabbath a little longer and not left until he could put the people behind him. Numbers 20:3 says that the people began to "chide" (*rib* or *rub*, #H7378) with Moses. This means to not only complain and argue, but to do it violently and very loudly! He had a few million people screaming at him, making the same complaints, in spite of the miraculous, in spite of the apparent blessing he was to them, in spite of God's will. Then they began to discount his care for them. They told him that his calling was a joke, and they didn't believe in him or the God that sent him. They were basically shouting that everything he had done for them was worthless. "We should have died when our brethren died and never left Egypt." They even went so far as to say that the promises and provisions of God were "evil."

In his anger, Moses went beyond disobeying God. He caused the power and presence of God to appear common before the people; and then he became arrogant. Moses didn't fail; he just dropped the ball for a minute. And God, over the course of time, would pick it up for him. He had a moment of indiscretion that dictated a change in his future. God still loved him and counted him as His friend, but now his destination would change.

Because we make a mistake doesn't mean we have failed. God's love for us is not contingent on our successes or failures. He loves us because we are His. But, despite all of that, He will not share His glory, and He has always been very specific about that. God would never forsake His friend, but his future would change now in order to preserve him.

The problem was that God told Moses to speak to the rock before the people, and He would bring water for the people and the animals. It was important to the Lord that the people had a living example of how it could be done. He wanted the people to know that they could trust Moses because Moses trusted God. The Lord wanted the people to be reminded that, "Yes, the Lord is with Moses; the favor of God is upon him. The God he walks with is alive and well. We can attempt to trust God the way Moses does." It was important that Moses lived out his spirituality in front of the people. After this incident, his gifts would stay intact, but his calling would forever be different.

It was important to the Lord then, as it is now, that our lives shout, not with words but with actions. God wasn't interested in exalting Moses; He was interested in being exalted through Moses in the most public of ways. When Moses said, "Must we fetch you water out of this rock?" he had brought himself to the place of being parallel with God. In all of his emotion, he was not careful, and arrogance lifted up its ugly head for the world to see.

The Word of God says that "pride goes before a fall." How many times has that been true in our lives? Probably too many to count! Remember the first rule of becoming a vessel—to do it not in our strength but in the Lord's strength. The day we begin to think that we have supernatural strength or power is the day we disqualify ourselves from operating in our gifts. Never allow anything to provoke you to attempt to be as God. There is only one God, and we are not Him. The Lord has pretty strict rules about His deity and glory:

He doesn't share them.

When we think that "God won't notice," that's when we begin to create our own rules, devoid of accountability and consequences. It is there that we imagine ourselves to be something that we are not, and it is there where we can pay the dearest of consequences for forgetting God is God, even for a brief moment.

When the consequences come upon your life, what do you do about them? Do you bury them and keep moving on? Or are you honest enough with God to stop your world and face the process of accountability held within that consequence? It's easy to move dirt around, but it's a little more complicated and delicate to tend a garden. Tend to the garden of your soul so that the consequences will have purpose instead of punishment. The consequences of Moses had great purpose; and because of that, he continued to emerge as a true friend of God.

CHAPTER 25

An Angry Root

*Then came the children of Israel, even the whole con-
gregation, into the desert of Zin in the first month: and
the people abode in Kadesh; and Miriam died there, and
was buried there. And there was no water for the congregation: and they gathered themselves together against
Moses and against Aaron. And the people chode with
Moses, and spake, saying, Would God that we had died
when our brethren died before the LORD! And why have
ye brought up the congregation of the LORD into this
wilderness, that we and our cattle should die there? And
wherefore have ye made us to come up out of Egypt, to
bring us in unto this evil place? It is no place of seed, or
of figs, or of vines, or of pomegranates; neither is there
any water to drink. And Moses and Aaron went from
the presence of the assembly unto the door of the tabernacle of the congregation, and they fell upon their faces:
and the glory of the LORD appeared unto them. And
the LORD spake unto Moses, saying, Take the rod, and
gather thou the assembly together, thou, and Aaron thy
brother, and speak ye unto the rock before their eyes; and
it shall give forth his water, and thou shalt bring forth to
them water out of the rock: so thou shalt give the congregation and their beasts drink. And Moses took the
rod from before the LORD, as he commanded him. And*

> *Moses and Aaron gathered the congregation together be-*
> *fore the rock, and he said unto them, Hear now, ye rebels;*
> *must we fetch you water out of this rock? And Moses lift-*
> *ed up his hand, and with his rod he smote the rock twice:*
> *and the water came out abundantly, and the congrega-*
> *tion drank, and their beasts also. And the LORD spake*
> *unto Moses and Aaron, Because ye believed me not, to*
> *sanctify me in the eyes of the children of Israel, therefore*
> *ye shall not bring this congregation into the land which*
> *I have given them. This is the water of Meribah; because*
> *the children of Israel strove with the LORD, and he was*
> *sanctified in them* (Numbers 20:1–13).

God is a God of truth, and He will not pretend He didn't see something when He did. He notices everything, and it's for our good. Moses would be far more fulfilled with the anger and arrogance completely gone. Nobody else could see it, but it was there, waiting to "happen" upon the next rock; and God was committed to helping His friend solve that problem.

The Last Bit of Egypt
Moses walked with amazing and miraculous results until his manhood came back upon him. When anger and arrogance found him, they would pull the last bit of Egypt out of him at the rock. This was not righteous indignation; it was pure and undefiled anger. Yes, the anger had been festering for many years, and when it came out it had wrinkles on it. But it still came, and Moses would have to be accountable for that. Not because of the anger, but because of how he presented himself before the people when he was angry. When we are angry, we are not trusting God, and we can make big mistakes against God and against our own lives. Moses was sanctified, and because of his anger, he refused to be seen that way. This was the last piece of Egypt in him, and it was trying to kill a rock in front of the whole world, while dragging Moses along for the ride. Sometimes the question isn't, "Have you loved the world?" but, "Have you let the world love you?" Often if we are not actively interacting

with the things of the world, we think that we have overcome them, but alas, the truth emerges from time to time: The world is hugging you desperately tight, and you don't seem to mind! Moses would learn how to peel the remnant of the world off himself and say, "No, I will not take comfort in you!"

Moses had been raised as the "prince of Egypt." We have seen earlier that he was "well trained in the ways of the Egyptians and was an eloquent speaker" back in the day. He was respected, revered and worshipped by many. Moses was the apparent heir to the throne and was educated and trained accordingly. More than half a lifetime of tending sheep and tramping through the wilderness evidently didn't get the "royal attitude" out of him, because the anger he displayed back at the brickyards in Egypt was the same anger that returned to visit him. Moses got confused in his role and made a huge mistake. But the mistake isn't what God was concerned about, God wanted to get Egypt out of Moses. God was willing to allow whatever it would take to get a pure vessel, because He knew that He could redeem it all and rescue His friend in the end, and He did.

The anger Moses displayed was not normal anger; it was birthed in arrogance and had been hidden for many years. It rose up in an attempt to destroy Moses, and God intervened to protect His friend.

Moses did something called "smote the rock" and he did it twice. I'm thinking these weren't small taps. Moses learned about "smiting" in Egypt. It was his "old self" making a comeback. You may think that smiting is no big deal, but "smote" (*nakah*, #H5221), according to the original Hebrew intent, here means "to strike (lightly or severely...) – beat...kill...slaughter...wound."

This is the same kind of "smote" that is used in Acts 7 when Stephen recalls the deeds of Moses in Egypt toward the Egyptian whom he killed: "And when he was full 40 years old, it came into his heart to visit his brethren, the children of Israel. And seeing one of them suffer wrong, he defended him and avenged him that was oppressed, and smote the Egyptian." The Egyptian died, and Moses buried him out back. When you are a "smoter," you usually have to hide your results and would rather not be seen in the light of them.

The "smote" that Moses engaged in while back in Egypt when he "smote the Egyptian" and killed him, is the same "smote" he used when he attacked the rock and smote it in front of all the people that he had been God's example to. He wanted someone to die a painful death, and God would have to intervene to save His friend from the angry, bitter root of his past. It would cost Moses Canaan—but he would gain more than the whole world and secure his friendship with God forever!

This type of "smoting" is used throughout the Word when someone is going to suffer grave and fatal consequences. And it's the smote that Moses employed as his weapon of choice because he wanted to do permanent damage. He had been leading the people and loving God through his wounds, and now the cause of those wounds manifested as anger.

He was mad, and he wanted to kill somebody. He needed them to feel pain all the way to their death. This anger was a trait of Egypt. It was not normal anger; it was Egyptian anger. If he couldn't get to somebody, he'd get to something. The same heart that killed the Egyptian was trying to kill the rock, but it really wanted to get its hands on the people. Moses left God behind as he said in Numbers 20:10, "Hear now, ye rebels; must we fetch you water out of this rock?" Moses left God out of the equation and elevated his anger above his ability to trust. He did it in front of the people that he and God had labored over for so long. God loved His friend, but He would have to stop the fury of Moses before it got out of control and he started killing people. Moses was in the middle of a meltdown, and God would save him from himself.

Notice that when Moses smote the rock, water flowed out of it, because that's who God is: faithful and full of provision. The water didn't just flow; it flowed abundantly. God is "faithful to complete and perform all these things He has spoken to us and to complete the work He has begun." Right in the middle of our anger and unbelief, right in the middle of arrogance and bad decisions, right in the middle of our mess and smoting, God is busy making a way!

Numbers 20:12 notes God speaking to Moses: "Because you believed me not, to sanctify me in the eyes of the children of Israel, therefore ye shall not bring this congregation into the land which I have given them." "Sanctify" (*qadash*, #H6942) here means "consecrate, dedicate…(be, keep) holy." The thing about God being sanctified in us is that He will not let who we were in our yesterdays cohabit with Him in our hearts today.

Moses had anger and arrogance hidden deep within his soul, and this was a part of Egypt that the Lord would have to get out of him to maintain their friendship. What is hidden in our hearts will either lead us into foolishness or into fellowship when times get hard. This was the critical moment for Moses. It was his "final surgery." Once God dealt with the anger and the arrogance, Moses would be home free. As soon as God took care of this issue in his heart, Moses would be consumed by God and delivered unto Him. That was fine with Moses because that's what he signed up for. When he said, "I want to see Your glory," in spite of the anger and arrogance that had crept in, he was asking to be made ready. When David said, "Find any wicked way in me," in spite of his lust for life, he was asking to be made ready. When Job "made sacrifice continually," in spite of his fear, he was asking to be made ready. When Esther said, "If I die, I die," in spite of her insecurities, she was asking to be made ready. Are you willing to pray the prayer of death over who you were to gain who He is and to be made ready?

Letting God Deal with It

It's a wonderful thing to allow the Lord to take not only your "skin, but your bones too." What's down deep are the honest portions of a person. I know a preacher who slammed his finger in a door and then he swore. I looked at him, and he said, "What? That hurt!" Okay, take a Sabbath, buddy! I told him that he had better take a little intermission from his mission so he could find out who God was in him. I told him his soul was provoking him to be something that God had called him out of. This man was a friend of God's, also, a wonderful man of God. But there was this thing, deep inside of him. God wanted it, and when it manifested, God wanted to grab it by the throat and kill it to protect his friend, this vessel of God. But this man decided that he was okay the way he was, and he didn't want God messing with him. Two years later he committed adultery, embezzled funds from his church, ran away, and we haven't heard from him since. He should have taken a Sabbath and prepared himself to be sanctified!

Walking in Spiritual Health

God was rescuing Moses from himself by taking "all that ails him" out. It seems like a painful surgery, but the recovery is quick and the spiritual health afterward is nothing short of awesome. God has a way of bringing "beauty for ashes" and rising up in our situations Himself to produce good things in us. For Romans still says, "All things work together for good." God is more concerned about the person than the ministry. He wants us more than what we can do for Him.

Because of Jesus, we are able to tear our walls down. Because of Jesus, we can live in restored favor and friendship with God. Because of Jesus, we are able to live as if "the rock" never happened and continue learning to trust Him. Because He lives, we live! We have opportunities every single day to overcome ourselves with the help of the Holy Spirit. We can choose yes or no. Our choices will determine the outcome of our lives; but even in that, God is still God, and will always love us and pick up the slack when we don't quite get the job done. Life is a continual journey of us getting up and falling down and getting up again. God is so faithful!

Maybe your efforts and purposes have taken a devastating toll on your life as you have disagreed with God or been unable to trust Him. Maybe your Canaan is long gone, and it's hard to imagine having passion about anything beyond what you can see today. Maybe you just don't know how to agree with God anymore, and the price seems too high. It is never too late, and He will always make a way; for these are the causes of Christ, and He will meet you as you reflect upon these pages.

When God is sanctified in us, we are saying that we are going to pay a little more attention. And when we don't, we fully expect God to intervene. In fact, we are counting on it, to preserve our friendship and fellowship with Him.

Sometimes the road of life feels too long and complicated, so we give up and settle for land that is easy to get to. Maybe you did that when you chose a nonconfrontational path, and now that path has grown teeth and claws and it's not as "user-friendly" as it was before. That's when God steps in and redefines who we are and sets us on a safe path, where friendship with Him is secure.

The long road to Canaan stretched out over many years, as tramping through the wilderness gave way to the making of a friend of God. The purpose of life is to become the friend of God and make His causes and desires our own. If we let Him, He will go to great lengths to make that happen. If we let Him, we shall see His glory and abide in His goodness. If we let Him, He will meet us right where we are and guide us through our desert into His abundant heart. If we let Him....

CHAPTER 26

Last Words

Moses is honored above many because he was able to trust God and call Him his Friend. Moses never cursed God and never gave up on God. He learned to follow and abide in a friendship that makes me crave that kind of fellowship.

In the New Testament, we see two men (who never saw death on this earth as we know it) at the transfiguration of Jesus Christ—Moses and Elijah. They appear in a position of honor to declare the greatest testimony that eternity would ever hold: "Jesus Christ, the Son of God, had become a man and would willingly lay His life down for the world." We hear Moses spoken of throughout the Word of God as the "friend" of God, who operated in trust and faith. He was the enduring, long-suffering vessel that would overcome himself to serve. He was the frail, rejected, insecure and fearful man who would dare to believe God was bigger than he was. He was an honored man, a faithful man, a man who got past his manhood. The time was approaching for Moses and would quickly come when the counter of the days on his life would come to a stop. The end of the story is surely greater than the beginning, and even in this, Moses would lay down before his God with an obedient heart; trusting Him, once again, for the outcome of the ages.

> *And the Lord said unto Moses, Get thee up into this mount Abarim, and see the land which I have given unto the*

children of Israel. And when thou hast seen it, thou also shalt be gathered unto thy people, as Aaron thy brother was gathered. For ye rebelled against my commandment in the desert of Zin, in the strife of the congregation, to sanctify me at the water before their eyes: that is the water of Meribah in Kadesh in the wilderness of Zin.

And Moses spake unto the Lord, saying, Let the Lord, the God of the spirits of all flesh, set a man over the congregation, Which may go out before them, and which may go in before them, and which may lead them out, and which may bring them in; that the congregation of the Lord be not as sheep which have no shepherd.

And the Lord said unto Moses, Take thee Joshua the son of Nun, a man in whom is the spirit, and lay thine hand upon him; And set him before Eleazar the priest, and before all the congregation; and give him a charge in their sight. And thou shalt put some of thine honour upon him, that all the congregation of the children of Israel may be obedient.

... And Moses did as the Lord commanded him: and he took Joshua, and set him before Eleazar the priest, and before all the congregation: And he laid his hands upon him, and gave him a charge, as the Lord commanded by the hand of Moses (Numbers 27:12–23).

Moses didn't ask God, "Why have You chosen this people, anyway? They hate You and they hate me!" Moses didn't defend himself by saying, "These people made me smote the rock because of all their complaining and chiding." He never even attempted a defense for himself, and he never blamed the people; he took full responsibility for what he had done. Somehow you feel that Moses was relieved that he was finally free of Egypt. There was no more bondage deep in his soul. The fight was over; he had become a sanctified vessel of honor, a true friend of God.

Once confession is made, we feel so much lighter and better. We don't care about the outcome, we just want the joy of true, honest freedom. Hiding behind a secret is a horrible way to live. Until Moses hit the rock, he had a secret—a secret of anger and arrogance. Once the truth came out, no matter what the consequences were, he would be a better man.

True to his friendship with his Lord, Moses was concerned only about what the Lord wanted. He didn't question the Lord's choice; he strove to accommodate it. God's desires had become his desires. That's why scripture says that the "Lord will give us the desires of our heart." When God's desires become our desires, it's easy.

The Last Words of Moses
At the end of his life, Moses was on the "way out" and only wanted one thing—for God's people to be taken care of. This was a beautiful declaration by a man who was selflessly consumed by his God. A rejected, wounded man could have never prayed that prayer. His request would have been riddled and afflicted with his own needs. When you are healed, you heal others; but when you are wounded, you wound others. Moses was done doing that. He would heal in the name of his God, through the heart of his God.

Your last request, your dying plea, the last words you will ever speak, and what do you ask for? You ask for God to bless the people whot have been driving you nuts for 40 years! That's selfless. It is very apparent that long before Moses was to breathe his last breath, the old man had already disappeared. He was a mere vapor, a thought of a man, for he was buried deep in the heart of God.

> *And Moses went and spake these words unto all Israel. And he said unto them, I am an hundred and twenty years old this day; I can no more go out and come in: also the Lord hath said unto me, Thou shalt not go over this Jordan. The Lord thy God, he will go over before thee, and he will destroy these nations from before thee, and thou shalt possess them: and Joshua, he shall go over before thee, as the Lord hath said. And*

the Lord shall do unto them as he did to Sihon and to Og, kings of the Amorites, and unto the land of them, whom he destroyed. And the Lord shall give them up before your face, that ye may do unto them according unto all the commandments which I have command-ed you. Be strong and of a good courage, fear not, nor be afraid of them: for the Lord thy God, he it is that doth go with thee; he will not fail thee, nor forsake thee (Deuteronomy 31:1–6).

Of all the things that Moses could have told Joshua, he said, "Be strong, don't be a coward, and don't be afraid!" He would later also tell him to be a man who knows the Word of God. So, this is the formula for success, and Joshua listened.

When somebody is saying their "last words" to you, it's always smart to pay attention. When God requires you to be the one say-ing the "last words" to someone else, you should pay attention. The problem is, we never know quite when those "last words" are go-ing to be uttered. So it's wisdom that whispers in our ear and re-minds us to pay attention to the Holy Spirit when He is speaking and hovering. People often ask how to come to the place of power and possession of authority in the Spirit of God. Two words: "Pay Attention." Listen when the Holy Spirit is talking to you.

But the anointing which ye have received of him abideth in you, and ye need not that any man teach you: but as the same anointing teacheth you of all things, and is truth, and is no lie, and even as it hath taught you, ye shall abide in him (1 John 2:27).

The Word isn't saying that you don't need a teacher, a pastor, a counselor or a friend. It is saying, "Concerning the intensity of the Spirit of God in you, concerning what the Lord would have you to do, listen to the Spirit that dwells in you. He will teach you how to behave in the Spirit, for He is Spirit. Pay attention!" Yes, it is a lost art form, but the "old school" is the best school. Simply "be still," so that you can "know that He is God" and don't forsake your Sabbath moments. He can always be found, for He is never far from you!

Daring to Believe

I was too busy to make a cake. And even if I wasn't too busy, I didn't feel like baking a cake. I just didn't want to! For a week the thought had tormented me, and I finally stopped and asked, "Okay, why do You want me to bake a cake, Lord?" All at once, I felt a need to give a cake to the man next door. "What kind of cake?"

"Chocolate—all chocolate, from the inside out, nothing but chocolate!" the Lord replied.

"Fine!"

I didn't know the man next door. He was older and stayed to himself. We had just moved into the neighborhood, and the week of our arrival his wife had died. The daughter came over and asked me if they could park cars in our driveway for the funeral.

So now, a few weeks later (I know, I know, I should have gone over sooner), I was baking this man a cake. A man who was a stranger and should never have been, for he was my neighbor. I am praying for him and shedding tears into the cake mix. I deliver the cake to the man, this very old and tired-looking man. He answered the door, and before he could snap out, "What do you want?" or, "Go away!" I volunteered these words: "I'm sorry for the loss of your wife. I know she must have loved you very much, and it's probably hard for you right now, but I have made you this cake to remind you that someone else loves you too. God loves you, and He has not forgotten about you, and He has not given up on you. Have a really nice day!"

I noticed his daughter in the background with her mouth hanging open. And then I turned and left. Deed done! I prayed for the man for a couple of days. I felt really sorry for him. His house was such a dark and lonely place. That's how life is without the Lord; it is dark and lonely.

Ten days later, the daughter came to my house to return my plate. She then asked if they could park cars in my driveway again. I asked her to come in. She explained to me the effect of my "last words."

She said that when I left that day, her dad was mad and wondered who I thought I was. But he didn't throw the cake away. He sat and looked at it for hours, she said, and she knew that he was pondering my words.

Then he dared to believe that what I had said was true. He cut the cake and wouldn't give his daughter any. He said that he was supposed to eat it. She said that each day, he took a piece of that cake and ate it and repeated the words that I told him when I handed it to him. He would say to himself, "God loves me and hasn't given up on me." She said he would say that over and over again. And one day, finally, he began to weep, and allowed the Holy Spirit to help him believe it.

He was a Christian when he and his wife were young. Their firstborn died, their only son; and although his wife had gone on, trusting God, this man couldn't stand the sound of God's name. He would get angry at his wife if she spoke of Jesus, and was a very bitter and lonely man because of it. The woman's prayer on her deathbed was that he would forgive God, but he wouldn't do it. Then, this stupid chocolate cake full of tears arrived, and God got him.

The daughter said that the day before he finished the cake, he asked God to forgive him, and the joy of the Lord returned to him. The day after he finished the cake, he died. Sweet redemption. You never know when you are the safety net beneath a life that has been shattered and torn.

Honesty Brings Redemption

Moses didn't miss the opportunity to take advantage of last words. He heard them and spoke them. When God told him to make the U-turn, he heard the words that God spoke. He didn't shrink back from them. When God is speaking something that we'd rather not hear, it's easy to pretend we didn't hear it. Go to the deep place in your heart and find the words that the Lord has spoken to you that you have forgotten, or refused to hear. Honesty brings redemption!

We had a dog once that we thought was deaf. The veterinarian said that the dog had perfect hearing—she just had a stubborn heart. When you said something she didn't want to hear, she just played deaf and dumb. Talk about an easy way out!

Don't take the path that is crowded with people who are trying to find a way to manipulate and control God. Take the path that has a few rocks on it, so you can have the pleasure of learning how to walk around them and enjoy the perfection of their placement on your road.

Moses spoke a blessing upon this people who tormented and tortured him for four decades. He was not dealing with forgiveness, because he didn't have to; he forgave them when they did it. You know you have forgiven someone when you can bless them! The last thing Moses did on his exit road was to bless the people.

> *And this is the blessing wherewith Moses the man of God blessed the children of Israel before his death. [He said,] The eternal God is thy refuge, and underneath are the everlasting arms: and he shall thrust out the enemy from before thee; and shall say, Destroy them. Israel then shall dwell in safety alone: the fountain of Jacob shall be upon a land of corn and wine; also his heavens shall drop down dew. Happy art thou, O Israel: who is like unto thee, O people saved by the Lord, the shield of thy help, and who is the sword of thy excellency! and thine enemies shall be found liars unto thee; and thou shalt tread upon their high places* (Deuteronomy 33:1, 27–29).

Moses has just spoken grand and glorious words of blessings over a people who have done nothing but grieve him. Because his heart is right and his friendship with God is intact, he is well able to do it and mean it!

The story of Moses is a grand and glorious testimony of a man who used to run. What an example of perseverance and trial! The friend of God just kept showing up, even when it looked like he was going to get the blame and the short end of the stick. He was ready to meet this One who had kept him all these years, the One he trusted to take him to the other side.

The arguments at the burning bush were long gone. The insecurities he had before Pharaoh had disintegrated under the weight of a mighty God. Here lies this friend, the one who yielded to God beyond himself, in order to walk in a friendship that could trust for anything. This Moses, the man who came to the decision that the Lord was all he really needed and the rest of life was a vapor, is speaking "last words" over us today and reminding us that life is not about Canaan, it's about that sweet friendship with the Lord along the journey.

What a bonus Moses received: "His eye was not dim, nor his natural force abated…." The consideration of God toward Moses went way beyond what we will ever know. God could work in Moses in "signs and wonders… and mighty terror with a mighty hand" because He trusted Moses. Friendship goes both ways, and when you are trusting God, you're letting Him know that you are trustworthy and He can trust you.

What have we done with God's desire to trust us with who He is? He is longing, as the Word says, to "show Himself strong in His people." Whatever is in the way of His desires becoming yours or His intentions coming to pass in your life, by now they have long outlived their usefulness.

I have grown so fond of Moses through these pages. Watching him evolve into a friend of God from a rejected, insecure, apathetic and depressed man has given me great hope that I, too, can walk in that kind of fellowship—the kind without boundaries or borders, that trusts with a reckless abandon.

And with that being said, Moses now takes his position as putty in the palm of God's hand: trusting the One who had won his heart so many years ago.

And what of you, dear reader? Have you come to the place where you are able to declare not only with your mouth but also with your life that Jesus is enough? No matter what life brings you, He must be enough! No matter what life has brought you, He must be enough! He is the prize and reward that lingers in our hearts long after our Egypt is destroyed and our Canaan taken away.

We have held each other through these pages and seen this mere man from Midian become a friend of God through trial and tragedy. I have hoped for you as you have advanced your way through the life of this man who holds history in his hand. Moses came to the place where he didn't care what speed the world was spinning; he was marching to his own drummer. Moses had the ability to "keep his eye on the mark of the prize." Once he got over himself, he didn't seem to care what the cost or consequence was to secure his fellowship with the One who would call him friend.

Have you arrived in that place? Are you able to let go of the rejection and insecurity that has held you hostage for so many years? Did you listen when the Holy Spirit was telling you that your controlling issues go way beyond organizational skills? Go to the place where faith becomes trust and trust becomes an honest declaration of not who you are, but who God is.

Canaan isn't the issue: it's that sweet little journey on the way to Canaan. Oh, how the days of the wilderness trek formed Moses and forged him into steel, causing him to be a trustworthy friend. In the end, you get the feeling that there is nothing that Moses couldn't hear God speak. Their fellowship and friendship became agreement and communion. Because of God's bravery and the willingness of Moses, God was able to "stop the train" at the rock and secure a better way for His friend. It was the way of secure and perfect fellowship that could not be shaken, for the very last piece of trouble and dismay had been removed from Moses's heart. He would live out the rest of his days without anger or arrogance. Therefore, when it was time for him to head on up to glory, his "last words" would carry weight and power because they were spoken by not only a purified man, but a sanctified one. God wasn't only sanctified in him anymore, but now Moses was also sanctified in God. He had successfully disappeared and melted into his God. No more would he react to the horrors of people, but only respond to the mandate of God. It cost him Canaan; but who cares, Canaan was never the prize, anyway. It was clearly a bus stop for Moses on his way to greatness in the arms of his God and Savior—his Friend!

> *Now faith is the substance of things hoped for, the evidence of things not seen. For by it the elders obtained a good report* (Hebrews 11:1–2).

I guess the question is: what report are you going for—the one that demands reality to be altered for your benefit or the one that says Jesus is enough? If you only go for faith, you will struggle; but if you are going for the report that comes from faith, the struggle is over. The report will determine what your heart was doing while your faith was trying to find trust.

> *And these all, having obtained a good report through faith, received not the promise: God having provided some better thing for us...* (Hebrews 11:39–40).

The "faith" here did not bring "the promise," but it brought the "good report," which would bring "some better thing." The "better thing" actually has nothing to do with the promise and everything to do with fellowship with Christ. True faith will not waver or obsess over Canaan, but will always be concerned with the journey of life as it relates to God and the opportunity to know Christ fully. True faith will set itself up to trust and recognize the price that was paid for fellowship and embrace it over everything else.

What attitude does your life reflect—relationship that says, "Give me that now!" or fellowship that says: "Give me what You have designed when You have ordained it to come." The people from Hebrews 11 never did receive the fulfillment of their promise here on the earth; they must have collected it on the "other side." So we know the fulfillment of a promise is not really about "getting it," but about abiding with Christ while we believe for it and all the "better things" that surround it!

Ask God what He wants so that you can willingly give it to Him, because abundance is on the other side of obedience. Shall it be milk and honey, or weeds and rocks for you? Even now He speaks to you of the beautiful treasure and privilege of the price of fellowship to gain friendship.

The Holy Spirit is hovering over your head right now, and He is whispering sweet words of favor upon you as you stand in agreement and awe of your Maker and Friend: Jesus Christ, the King of Glory.

Be blessed by your abundantly faithful Friend as you go forward with Him, hand-in-hand, to abide where friendship is forged through life.

As we have traveled this road with Moses, one thing is abundantly clear: God will always pull us toward His heart. As we yield to Him, instead of acting out our rejections and lack of trust, we will be able to hear Him inviting us to come to that secret place with Him.

As the ages cease upon the life of our friend, Moses, let us pray the prayer that could have been on his heart as he laid his head down in the hand of the One he trusted—his God and his Friend.

Lord, throughout the pages of my life, You have captured my soul with Your loving-kindness and shown me Your heart. Thank You for being consumed with me and not my performance. As my soul gazes into the heavens, I know without doubt that You love me, not because of the way things have turned out, but because You have never left me. Amen.

References

Albright, Joe. "Just Stay in the Race." *Daily Messages*. January 9, 2021. https://www.dialhope.org/just-stay-in-the-race-2/.

Drake, Sir Francis. "Disturb Us, Lord." Renovaré. Accessed November 2, 2023. https://renovare.org/articles/disturb-us-lord.

Merriam-Webster.com Dictionary. https://www.merriam-webster.com/.

New American Standard Exhaustive Concordance with Hebrew-Aramic and Greek Dictionaries. The Lockman Foundation. 1981, 1998. Bible Hub online, https://biblehub.com/.

Strong, James. *Strong's Exhaustive Concordance* online. Bible Hub. https://biblehub.com/strongs.htm.

Vine, W.E. *Vine's Expository Dictionary of Old & New Testament Words*. Nashville, Tennessee: Thomas Nelson Publishers, 1997.

About the Author

S andra Hardister Querin was called at the age of nine to "prepare for the day" when she would preach the Good News. Although hampered by cystic fibrosis for 30 years, she pursued the call of God and her education, holding an MBA, JD, MDiv and ThD. She married her high school sweetheart and was married for 45 years. Sandi was a college professor and corporate executive along with serving on staff of several churches until the Lord called her into full-time ministry.

Supernaturally healed of her disease, she walks in miraculous healing power that is predominately prophetic. The cry of her heart is for the lost to be saved and for the saved to be empowered by Jesus Christ.

Sandi travels the world spreading the Gospel and bringing hope to the hurting and healing to the broken. The sick come to her meetings for their miracles and are not disappointed, because Jesus does not disappoint. Sandi serves as the lead pastor at The Revival Center in Clovis, California. You can follow the services online or find out more about Sandi and her ministry at: www.Abbasheart.com.

She enjoys her children and grandchildren when she is not traveling and serves as a Fresno County chaplain.

The Prayer of Donny is the third book in the Honest to God Series, following *The Prayer of Job* and *The Prayer of Moses*.

You can contact the author at:
1516 Draper Street, Kingsburg, CA 93631
559.897.9575
Sandi@abbasheart.com

www.ingramcontent.com/pod-product-compliance
Lightning Source LLC
Chambersburg PA
CBHW070917120626
46546CB00001B/301